SANDWICH RECIPES BOOK

The Sandwich Cookbook for All Things Sweet and Wonderful!

(A Chicken Sandwich Cookbook for Effortless Meals)

Cleveland Harkless

Published by Alex Howard

© Cleveland Harkless

All Rights Reserved

Sandwich Recipes Book: The Sandwich Cookbook for All Things Sweet and Wonderful! (A Chicken Sandwich Cookbook for Effortless Meals)

ISBN 978-1-990169-51-9

All rights reserved. No part of this guide may be reproduced in any form without permission in writing from the publisher except in the case of brief quotations embodied in critical articles or reviews.

Legal & Disclaimer

The information contained in this book is not designed to replace or take the place of any form of medicine or professional medical advice. The information in this book has been provided for educational and entertainment purposes only.

The information contained in this book has been compiled from sources deemed reliable, and it is accurate to the best of the Author's knowledge; however, the Author cannot guarantee its accuracy and validity and cannot be held liable for any errors or omissions. Changes are periodically made to this book. You must consult your doctor or get professional medical advice before using any of the suggested remedies, techniques, or information in this book.

Table of contents

PART 1 1

CHAPTER 1: BREAKFAST SANDWICHES 2

RECIPE 1: CHEESE, EGG 'N BACON BREAKFAST SANDWICH 2
RECIPE 2: BREAKFAST GRILLED CHEESE EGGS SANDWICH 5
RECIPE 3: FRUIT ENGLISH MUFFIN SANDWICH 7
RECIPE 4: HOT HAM 'N CHEESE CROISSANT SANDWICH 9
RECIPE 5: COFFEE SHOP COPYCAT BREAKFAST SANDWICH 11

CHAPTER II - LUNCH AND DINNER SANDWICHES 13

RECIPE 6: SMOKED SALMON PEPPER-JACK SANDWICH 13
RECIPE 7: QUICK EASY BARBEQUE SANDWICH 15
RECIPE 8: GOAT CHEESE CUCUMBER SANDWICH 17
RECIPE 9: TURKEY PROVOLONE SANDWICH 19
RECIPE 10: CRAB-LEMON SANDWICH 21
RECIPE 11: OPEN-FACE APPLE-HAM SANDWICH 23
RECIPE 12: TURKEY SLIDER 25
RECIPE 13: CUCUMBER SUB SANDWICH 27
RECIPE 14: TUNA RED PEPPER SANDWICH 29
RECIPE 15: PESTO PANINI 30
RECIPE 16: LOW-CARB SUBMARINE LETTUCE-WICH 32
RECIPE 17: COFFIN SANDWICH 34
RECIPE 18: CAESAR SALAD SANDWICH 36
RECIPE 19: MEATLOAF SANDWICH 38
RECIPE 20: GOAT CHEESE NIBBLER TEA SANDWICH 39
RECIPE 21: QUINTESSENTIAL EGG SANDWICH 41
RECIPE 22: SPINACH, HUMMUS 'N TOMATO SANDWICH 43

RECIPE 23: MEATBALL SUB SANDWICH 45

RECIPE 24: SPIDER SANDWICH 47

RECIPE 25: TURKEY, CREAM CHEESE 'N CRANBERRY SANDWICH 49

CHAPTER III - DESSERT SANDWICHES 51

RECIPE 26: BANANA FLUFF SANDWICH 51

RECIPE 27: MONKEY TOAST SANDWICH 52

RECIPE 28: CREAM CHEESE BERRY SANDWICH 54

RECIPE 29: GRANOLA APPLE-WICH 56

RECIPE 30: EASY ICE CREAM SANDWICH 58

PULLED PORK AND KALE BISCUIT SANDWICHES 61

CHICKEN PARM SLIDERS 63

SLOW-COOKER FRENCH DIP 64

EGG IN A HOLE BREAKFAST SANDWICH 65

CHICKEN PARM SUB 67

CHIMICHURRI STEAK SANDWICH 69

GRILLED CHEESE WITH TOMATOES AND BACON 71

ITALIAN CLUB 72

HASH BROWN BREAKFAST SANDWICHES 74

SRIRACHA MEATLOAF 76

CHICKEN AND WAFFLES BREAKFAST SANDWICH 78

EGG IN A HOLE BLT 80

BREAKFAST BURGER 81

CHICKEN MEATBALL SLIDERS WITH MOZZARELLA AND WILTED SPINACH 84

OPEN-FACED BACON AVOCADO TOMATO SANDWICH 86

BONUS: LEMONY CRAB ROLLS 87

PART 2 88

CHAPTER 1: ABC SANDWICH 89

Acapulco Fishburgers 90

Alaska Salmon Salad Sandwich 91

CHAPTER 2: AVOCADO CHICKEN MELT 93

Couzan Billy Burger 94

Crescent Monte Cristo Loaf 96

Chili Dog Rolls 97

CHAPTER 3: BAKED PIZZA SANDWICH 99

All-American Barbecue Sandwiches 101

Fired Up Over Turkey Barbeque,"Grilled Crab Sandwich 102

CHAPTER 4: TEXAS BARBECUE SANDWICH 103

Italian Pork Sandwiches 104

Submarine Sandwich 105

Roasted Red Pepper Stuffed Sandwich 107

CHAPTER 5: PALM BEACH SANDWICHES (A.K.A. PIMENTO CHEESE SANDWICHES) 108

Jumbo Party Sandwich 110

Ham Salad 112

Ham And Cheese Party Loaf 113

German-Style Ham Sandwich 115

CHAPTER 6: EGG SALAD SPREAD SUPREME 116

Creamy Chicken And Braeburn Apple Sandwiches 117

Chicken-Vegetable Salad Filling 119

Nola Rib-Eye Sandwich 120

Garlic Meatball Po'boys 122

WHY SANDWICHES ARE BENEFICIAL FOR YOU 125

DELICIOUS SANDWICH RECIPES 127

RECIPE 1: LOADED TURKISH STYLE GRILLED CHEESE 127
RECIPE 2: HEALTHY STIR-FRIED VEGGIE SANDWICH 130
RECIPE 3: ROASTED SWEET POTATO SANDWICH WITH RAJAS SALSA 133
RECIPE 4: CLASSIC MONTE CRISTO 135
RECIPE 5: FILLING PORK BELLY GYRO 137
RECIPE 6: ITALIAN STYLE PULLED PORK SANDWICH 140
RECIPE 7: TUNA AND LEMON CAPER SANDWICH 144
RECIPE 8: FILLING SPAM AND CHEESE SANDWICH 147
RECIPE 9: TASTY PIMENTO CHEESE SANDWICH WITH HOMEMADE PICKLES 149
RECIPE 10: CALIFORNIA STYLE SANDWICH 152
RECIPE 11: SALVADORAN TURKEY SANDWICH 154
RECIPE 12: BRAZILIAN STYLE ROAST BEEF SANDWICH... 157
RECIPE 13: FRIED MOZZARELLA SANDWICHES 159
RECIPE 14: SIMPLE HONEY AND RICOTTA SANDWICH.. 161
RECIPE 15: BUTTERMILK STYLE FRIED CHICKEN SANDWICH 163
RECIPE 16: SIMPLE TOMATO SANDWICH 166
RECIPE 17: CHICKEN SCHNITZEL SANDWICH SMOTHERED IN HORSERADISH CREAM AND RADICCHIO 168
RECIPE 18: HEARTY PORCHETTA SANDWICHES... 171
RECIPE 19: BEL AIR STYLE CLUB SANDWICH 175
RECIPE 20: SOFT CRAB SANDWICH SMOTHERED WITH COLLARD SLAW 178
RECIPE 21: JERSEY STYLE PORK ROLL BREAKFAST SANDWICH 181
RECIPE 22: FILLING LEMON, HAM AND CHEESE SANDWICHES 183
RECIPE 23: CLASSIC FOOTBALL SANDWICHES 186
RECIPE 24: CUBAN STYLE MEDIANOCHE SANDWICH 188
RECIPE 25: TASTY SMOTHERED PIMENTO CHEESE BRAISED BRISKET SANDWICHES 190

Part 1

Chapter 1: Breakfast Sandwiches

Recipe 1: Cheese, Egg 'N Bacon Breakfast Sandwich

Breakfast sandwiches reign supreme over many other types of breakfast choices. You probably won't be able to isolate any one ingredient that Makes this sandwich good for a hangover cure or meal on the go choice. Could it be the bacon or egg? Or the choice of croissant, bagel or biscuit? This cheese, egg and bacon classic will be folded inside pastry dough for what amounts to a breakfast calzone.

Yield: 6 Servings

Preparation Time: 55 minutes

Ingredient List:
- 10 lightly beaten eggs, large
- 2 packets of dry yeast, active
- 4 cups of cheddar cheese, grated
- 1 ½ pound of sliced bacon, a bit crispy
- 1 3/4 cups of flour, all-purpose

- ¼ teaspoons of sugar, granulated
- ½ teaspoons of salt, and more as desired
- Black pepper, ground, as desired
- Olive oil to brush on
- Semolina to dust with

Preparation:

1. Combine 3/4 cup of water at 115F with yeast and sugar in medium bowl. Allow to sit until the mixture becomes foamy. This should take between 8-10 minutes.

2. Whisk salt and flour in another bowl. Add the yeast mixture created in step 1. The result should have a consistency like dough.

3. Transfer to floured cutting board. Knead until dough is elastic and smooth. This will take just a few minutes.

4. Use plastic wrap to cover dough. Set it aside for 8-12 minutes.

5. Heat oven to 450F. Mix the eggs, cheese, bacon, salt pepper in medium bowl.

6. Divide the dough into six balls. Work in two batches of three balls each. Roll them into eight-inch rounds. They should be no more than 1/8 of an inch thick.

7. Place 3/4 cup of the egg mixture on one side of all rounds. Leave a one-inch border around the mixture. Fold the other halves of the rounds over. Pinch the edges to seal in the mixture completely.

8. Transfer your calzones to a pre-dusted (with semolina) pan. Brush tops of calzones using olive oil. Slide the calzones into oven. Bake for 15 to 20 minutes, until they are golden in color.

9. Repeat steps with the rest of the dough balls and the remainder of the egg mixture. Remove from stove. Serve hot.

Recipe 2: Breakfast Grilled Cheese Eggs Sandwich

Grilled cheese is a classic comfort sandwich, often served alongside a steamy bowl of soup. But you can also add eggs and kale, as this recipe does, to make it greener and healthier. Kale is a superfood, and grilled cheese is already a super sandwich. Call it whatever you like, but you'll be hooked.

Yield: 2 Servings

Preparation Time: 40 minutes

Ingredient List:
- 3 eggs, large
- Butter to spread, softened
- 6 oz. of grated Havarti cheese
- 4 slices of bread, wheat or white
- 1 tablespoon of mustard, Dijon
- 3 tablespoons of mayonnaise
- 1 head of curly kale, torn from the stems
- ¼ teaspoons of paprika, smoked
- ¼ teaspoons of red pepper flakes, crushed

- ¼ teaspoons of salt, kosher
- ¼ teaspoons of pepper, ground

Preparation:

1. Preheat oven to 350F. Place kale on cookie sheet. Spritz with coconut or olive oil. Sprinkle with kosher salt ground pepper, then pepper flakes. Roast kale for 8-10 minutes. Toss lightly. Roast for 10 more minutes until barely crispy.

2. Stir paprika, mayo and mustard together.

3. Spread outsides of slices of bread with soft butter. Spread insides with the mixture including mayo. Top all slices with cheese.

4. Heat skillet on med. heat. Place bread with buttered side facing down. Cook all like open-faced sandwiches. This keeps the kale nice and crispy.

5. While they are toasting, heat a separate skillet on med. heat. Fry eggs.

6. Remove all from heat. Top two slices of cheesy toast with kale. Other slices will be the top. Toss an egg on top of each one. Serve warm.

Recipe 3: Fruit English Muffin Sandwich

When you top buttery, crisp toasted English muffins with fresh fruit and cream cheese, peanut butter or yogurt, you get an unbeatable breakfast. These sandwiches offer you an easy and fun way to prepare your first meal of the day.

Yield: 1 Serving

Preparation Time: 10 minutes

Ingredient List:
- 1 English muffin
- Options for spread – pick one or more
- Marshmallow fluff
- Mashed avocado
- Chocolate hazelnut spread
- Cream cheese (whipped) with powdered sugar
- Greek yogurt
- Peanut butter, creamy
- Options for topping
- Chopped nuts

- Apple slices
- Kiwi slices
- Banana slices
- Blueberries
- Raspberries
- Blackberries
- Strawberries

Preparation:

1. Cut an English muffin in half.
2. Spread the bottom part with your chosen spread.
3. Arrange your favorite toppings on the spread.
4. Pop the other half of your muffin on top. Serve.

Recipe 4: Hot Ham 'N Cheese Croissant Sandwich

These are croque monsieurs with a unique twist. Those are hot ham cheese sandwiches that are topped with white sauce and extra cheese. These sandwiches are made with croissants, instead of bread. It's not health food, to be sure, but the taste is so great, you probably won't care.

Yield: 4 Servings

Preparation Time: 40 minutes

Ingredient List:
- 8 oz. of thinly sliced honey ham
- Mustard, Dijon
- 8 croissants
- 2 cups of milk, hot
- ½ cup of Parmesan, grated
- 12 oz. of grated Gruyere cheese
- 3 tablespoons of flour, all-purpose
- 2 tablespoons of butter, unsalted

- 1 teaspoon of salt, kosher
- ½ teaspoons of black pepper, ground
- 1 pinch of nutmeg

Preparation:

1. Preheat oven to 400F.

2. Melt butter in sauce pan on low heat. Add flour. Stir for about two minutes.

3. Pour hot milk slowly into flour-butter mixture. Whisk constantly while cooking, until sauce has become thicker.

4. Remove from heat. Add Parmesan, ½ cup Gruyere, nutmeg, salt and pepper. Set aside.

5. Cut croissants in half. Place on baking sheets. Bake for three to five minutes. Turn over and bake for two more minutes. They should be just barely toasted.

6. Brush ½ of croissants lightly with mustard. Add ham slice to each one. Sprinkle with ½ of remaining Gruyere cheese. Top with other halves.

7. Slather tops with cheese sauce and sprinkle remaining Gruyere.

8. Bake sandwiches for four to six minutes.

9. Turn on broiler. Broil for three to five minutes. Tops should be lightly browned and bubbly. Serve them hot.

Recipe 5: Coffee Shop Copycat Breakfast Sandwich

This delectable breakfast feast on rolls is so easy, and it tastes just as good as the sandwiches at that coffee place you see on virtually any corner. In addition, after you build and assemble them, you can wrap them and store in the freezer. Then you can grab one whenever you like and just pop it in the microwave – instant goodness.

Yield: 4 Servings

Preparation Time: 25 minutes

Ingredient List:
- 4 slices of cheese, Swiss or Gouda
- 4 rolls, Ciabatta
- 4 slices of bacon, crispy
- 2 tablespoons of milk, 2%
- 1 tablespoon of Parmesan cheese, grated
- 4 eggs, large
- 1 pinch of salt, kosher
- 1 pinch of pepper, black

Preparation:

1. Preheat the oven to 375F.

2. Grease four holes on muffin pan.

3. Beat salt, pepper, milk, parmesan and eggs together until they appear frothy. Divide the mixture between the muffin cups. Bake for 8-12 minutes. They should be set and puffed when done.

4. Cook bacon. Slice Ciabatta rolls open.

5. Set the open rolls on cookie sheet. When egg mixture has cooked, remove from pan. Arrange on bottoms of rolls. Add cheese and then bacon. Put the tray in oven. Broil only long enough that the cheese begins to melt. Serve hot.

Chapter Ii - Lunch And Dinner Sandwiches

Recipe 6: Smoked Salmon Pepper-Jack Sandwich

This sandwich includes what you will find is among the best salmon you've ever had. It is rubbed with maple syrup and brown sugar. It even SOUNDS tasty. The unique taste lends itself well to lunch or dinner sandwiches. Your family will eat more healthy salmon if you cue up this recipe once a week or so.

Yield: 1 Serving

Preparation Time: 15 minutes

Ingredient List:
- 2 slices of your favorite bread
- 1 slice of tomato, fresh
- 1 fried egg
- 1 slice of cheese, pepper jack
- ¼ lb. of flaked salmon, smoked

Preparation:

1. Toast 2 bread slices. On one, layer salmon, tomato, egg and cheese slice.

2. Place under a preheated broiler, just until the cheese has melted. Top with second slice of bread. Serve.

Recipe 7: Quick Easy Barbeque Sandwich

These barbeque sandwiches are simply one of the easiest meals to make. Your youngster could probably make them. (Safety note – don't let your children make hot sandwiches alone.) Just put the beef in a slow cooker with beef broth and cook low and slowly. Get some work done or watch some binge-worthy TV while it cooks. When you remove the beef from the slow cooker and shred it, you're ready to add any favorite barbeque sauce. Then let the beef heat a half-hour longer. It's easy and delicious.

Yield: 6 Servings

Preparation Time: 8 hours and 10 minutes

Ingredient List:
- Colby jack or cheddar cheese, sliced
- 6 buns, hamburger
- 3/4 cup of barbeque sauce, your fav
- 1 x 14 ½ ounce can of broth, beef

- 3-pound chuck roast

Preparation:

1. Place the roast in a crock pot. Pour the broth in on top. Cook on a low setting for about eight hours.

2. Remove the roast from the crock pot. Place it on cutting board. Shred the beef using a fork and tongs or two forks.

3. Empty the broth from the crock pot. Place beef in pot once again. Pour the barbeque sauce over the beef. Toss and coat the beef evenly with the sauce.

4. Cook in crock pot on low for a half-hour longer. The meat should be heated all the way through. Remove from crock pot and place on buns. Top with cheese. Serve hot.

Recipe 8: Goat Cheese Cucumber Sandwich

These little sandwiches are great for brunch or lunch. Use slices of thinly-sliced, soft bread. The tastes play off each other in an interesting way and you will be surprised at how tasty this sandwich is.

Yield: 9 Servings

Preparation Time: 25 minutes

Ingredient List:
- 12 slices bread, wheat or white
- ½ sliced cucumber
- ½ teaspoons of fresh chives, chopped
- 2 oz. of cream cheese
- 2 oz. of cheese, goat

Preparation:

1. Mix chives and cheeses together. Use salt pepper to season if desired.

2. Spread 12 bread slices with cheese mixture. Layer cucumber slices atop cheese mixture. Layer them a bit.

3. If you want some closed sandwiches, as opposed to all open-faced, top six of the sandwiches with remaining bread slices.

4. Use a cookie cutter to press down through the bread and toppings until you have cut completely through the sandwiches.

5. Arrange sandwiches on a dainty plate. Serve. They go especially well with white wine or a spot of tea.

Recipe 9: Turkey Provolone Sandwich

These open-faced sandwiches are a quick and filling dinner, before you head off for any evening activities you have planned. It's really a surprise. It doesn't just taste great – it's also deceptively easy to make. The flavors have a nice depth, and complement each other so well.

Yield: 6 Servings

Preparation Time: 30 minutes

Ingredient List:

- 6 slices of cheese, provolone
- 3/4 cup of drained, dried pepper, red
- 1 ½ loaves of frozen garlic bread, thawed
- 1 ½ cups of fresh baby spinach

Preparation:

1. Bake the garlic bread using the instructions on the package.

2. Layer bread with turkey, then spinach, then red peppers, then cheese.

3. Bake for several minutes longer. The cheese should melt well.

4. Cut into pieces. Serve.

Recipe 10: Crab-Lemon Sandwich

If you haven't eaten soft-shell crabs, check them out the next time they are featured at your local market. You might find it interesting to make these sandwiches. Most recipes use deep-fried shell crabs, and this recipe adds coleslaw and mustard aioli. The soft-shell crab has sweeter taste than many other types of shellfish, so it fits this sandwich well.

Yield: 8 Servings

Preparation Time: 25 minutes

Ingredient List:
- 3 sliced tomatoes, ripe
- 8 lettuce leaves
- 8 hot dog buns or rolls
- ½ cup of mayo
- 1 lemon, juice only
- 2 diced stalks of celery
- 2 bunches of sliced green onions, light green white parts only

- 2 lbs. of crab meat, coked
- ½ teaspoons of salt, kosher
- ¼ teaspoons of pepper, black

Preparation:

1. Go through the crab meat by hand. Discard any shell pieces. Chop meat finely.

2. Combine the crab meat, salt pepper, mayo, lemon juice, celery and green onions in medium bowl.

3. Toast rolls until they are just starting to brown.

4. Spoon some chilled crab meat mixture on ½ of the rolls. Place tomatoes and lettuce on other ½. Serve promptly.

Recipe 11: Open-Face Apple-Ham Sandwich

Want to make a simple after school snack or lunch for yourself or your family? Use French bread, apples, deli meat and any cheese you have in the fridge to make this classic sandwich. It's very yummy and ticks off many food groups. There is something on this sandwich for everyone in the home to enjoy, so it's suitable for all tastes.

Yield: 4 Servings

Preparation Time: 20 minutes

Ingredient List:
- ¼ cup of mozzarella cheese, shredded
- ¼-pound of ham, deli
- 1 sliced apple
- ¼ loaf of bread, French

Preparation:

1. Cut the bread into ¼-inch slices. Layer with apple slices first, followed by the ham and then the mozzarella cheese. The number of slices varies, depending on the size of the loaf.

2. Bake at 390F in a toaster oven for about six to eight minutes. Cheese should begin showing brown bubbles.

3. Remove from the toaster oven using hot pads. Serve warm or hot.

Recipe 12: Turkey Slider

Sliders are like burgers that are more fun, and these will brighten up a dinner. They offer twice the patties and twice the crunchy, creamy slaw. Choose plain ground turkey instead of turkey breast, if you want to save on fat calories. The dark meat tends to have a leaner profile, too. The chilies have a mild or medium heat, which gives the sliders oomph. Sweet bell peppers can be substituted, if you prefer.

Yield: 4 Servings (2 sliders each)

Preparation Time: 20 minutes

Ingredient List:
- 8 toasted slider buns, whole wheat
- 1 sliced cucumber, small
- 2 tablespoons of lime juice, fresh
- ¼ cup of mayonnaise, canola
- ½ cup of apple, chopped
- 1 cup of coleslaw mix, shredded
- 1 lb. of turkey, ground

- ½ teaspoons of cumin, ground
- ¼ teaspoons of red pepper, ground
- ½ teaspoons of salt, kosher

Preparation:

1. Preheat the oven broiler with the rack in upper middle slot.

2. Combine cumin, salt, red pepper and ground turkey in medium mixing bowl. Divide. Shape the turkey mixture into eight x two-inch wide patties.

3. Arrange the patties on non-greased cookie sheet. Broil for two to three minutes on both sides.

4. Combine juice, mayo, apple and shredded coleslaw mix in a separate bowl. Divide the cucumbers on the bottom of buns. Top with turkey patties, the coleslaw mixture and then the tops of the buns. Serve.

Recipe 13: Cucumber Sub Sandwich

Want to switch up lunch with something more interesting? There are so many different ways to think outside the bun – or the bread – for breadless sandwiches. Sandwich bread is full of carbs and about 90 calories per slice. You can certainly do better. This sub uses cucumber instead of bread. You might pause at the thought of cucumber as a bread substitute, but it's so tasty.

Yield: 2 Servings

Preparation Time: 10 minutes

Ingredient List:
- Cream cheese or mayonnaise
- Deli meat – ham or turkey
- 2 cucumbers, large
- Green onions
- tomatoes
- bacon
- sandwich fillers, as desired

Preparation:

1. Cut cucumber length-ways. Scoop inside flesh out, so that there will be plenty of room for the fillings.

2. Add the meat and vegetables, and any other makings on the inside of cucumber. Place the other ½ of the cucumber on top. Serve.

Recipe 14: Tuna Red Pepper Sandwich

Sandwiches come in so many different styles. This is a variation on tuna sandwiches. The roasted peppers lend it sweetness, but the watercress gives it a bite of pepper. If you prefer, you can use arugula or baby spinach, too.

Yield: 4 Servings

Preparation Time: 10 minutes

Ingredient List:

- 1 teaspoon of vinegar, red wine
- ¼ cup of basil leaves, chopped
- 1/3 cup of sliced red peppers, roasted
- 1 tablespoon of olive oil, extra virgin
- 2 x 6-ounce cans of water-packed tuna
- ¼ teaspoons of pepper, ground

Preparation:

1. Combine the olive oil, pepper, tuna, vinegar, peppers and basil leaves. Spread this on your preferred type of roll or bread. Serve. How easy was that?

Recipe 15: Pesto Panini

Beef panini is a magical type of sandwich. It turns a plain roast beef sandwich (and those are good, too, make no mistake) into a tempting meal, when you brush it with oil and press it on stovetop grilling pan. It's so simple, but so satisfying at the same time. You can use any kind of cheese you like. Paninis are a favorite sandwich and these are SO tasty.

Yield: 2 Servings

Preparation Time: 20 minutes

Ingredient List:

- 2 slices of cheese, mozzarella
- 2 tablespoons of butter, unsalted
- 4 slices of deli roast beef
- 1 teaspoon of pesto, basil
- 2 slices of bread, rye

Preparation:

1. Spread the butter on a single side of each bread slice.
2. Place the bread with buttered side facing down in fry pan on med. heat.
3. Put slices of mozzarella on the slices of bread. Allow the cheese to melt fully.
4. Once the cheese is melted, place the roast beef on top of it.
5. Spread the pesto on other slices of bread. Place them on top of roast beef, making sandwiches. Place other slices on top of pesto.
6. Flip sandwich over and toast the other side. Allow the other slice of bread to become brown. This will take just a couple minutes. Serve hot.

Recipe 16: Low-Carb Submarine Lettuce-Wich

This is the ultimate low or no-carb sandwich, since there is no bread. Instead, it uses lettuce, and it doesn't get much less carb-dense than that. Eating breadless sandwiches is a trend today, especially for people seeking sandwiches and snacks that are lower in carbs. This sub lettuce-wich is very easy to make, and the taste will surprise you, in a good way.

Yield: 4 Servings

Preparation Time: 25 minutes

Ingredient List:

- 1 tablespoon of mayonnaise
- 2 oz. of sliced cheese, Swiss
- 6 ounces of sliced roast beef
- 2 lettuce leaves (romaine)
- Black pepper, ground
- Vinegar, just a spritz

Preparation:

1. Lay the lettuce leaves out on a medium plate. Spread each leaf with ½ of the mayonnaise. Add vinegar and black pepper.

2. Lay meat and cheese out on each lettuce leaf.

3. Put both halves of lettuce leaves together. Wrap in paper towels. Serve promptly.

Recipe 17: Coffin Sandwich

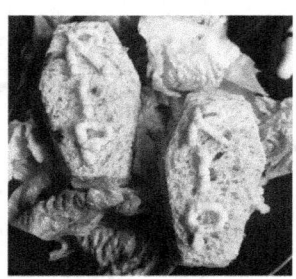

This is quite a unique sandwich, and one your kids or kids-at-heart will love. You will be removing the crusts, which kids instinctively tear off themselves anyway. And it's shaped like a coffin, which is cute. You don't need a coffin cookie cutter – just use a knife.

Yield: 2 Servings

Preparation Time: 15 minutes

Ingredient List:

- 2 leaves of lettuce
- 2 tablespoons of mayonnaise
- 2 pieces of cheese, your choice on type
- 6 slices of deli ham
- 4 slices of bread, whole-wheat

Preparation:

1. Cut the slices of bread into coffin shapes. You can make a template in the shape of a coffin out of cardboard, or just free-style cut out the shape.

2. Layer the sandwiches with meat, cheese, lettuce and dressing. Spear the sandwiches with plastic toothpicks to hold them together, as desired. Serve.

Recipe 18: Caesar Salad Sandwich

A Caesar salad doesn't seem like something that would be easy to make, let alone making one as a sandwich. But it's not difficult to make at all. Just throw the lettuce together with dressing, place them on a roll and top with Parmesan and chicken. You can add a little bit of extra dressing, too. To make this dish even simpler, you can buy pre-cooked and cut chicken breast strips at the grocery.

Yield: 1 Servings

Preparation Time: 15 minutes

Ingredient List:
- 3 tablespoons of Parmesan cheese, shredded
- 1 oz. of chicken breast, roasted strips
- 2 tablespoons of salad dressing, Caesar
- 1 cup of chopped lettuce
- 1 sandwich roll

Preparation:

1. Add lettuce, then Caesar salad dressing to a medium mixing bowl. Toss and combine.

2. Open sandwich roll. Add lettuce Caesar dressing mixture to bottom of roll.

3. Add roasted, sliced chicken breast and then top the meat using Parmesan cheese.

4. Close sandwich with another half of roll. Serve.

Recipe 19: Meatloaf Sandwich

You'll find that meatloaf can be a lot like the turkey you make for Thanksgiving. It's even better the next day – or at least it is when it's pressed between two bread slices. To build the perfect sandwich, you'll want to remember that for this recipe, you need white bread. Meatloaf just seems to taste its best when the bread is square, white and moist.

Yield: 2 Servings

Preparation Time: 10 minutes

Ingredient List:
- 2 slices of cooked meat loaf
- 4 leaves of lettuce
- 4 slices of roll or hoagie
- 2 tablespoons of mayonnaise

Preparation:

1. Spread mayo on two slices of bread. Top with meatloaf and lettuce. Serve.

Recipe 20: Goat Cheese Nibbler Tea Sandwich

This is not necessarily about the old-time ladies' teas, where all the guests wore white gloves and hats while nibbling on tiny sandwiches. But this sandwich would fit right in at those old teas. And now you can see these teas once more in hotels and homes. These thoroughly modern tea sandwiches are less sweet than savory, and go equally well with Earl Gray tea or a drink of something harder.

Yield: 24 Servings

Preparation Time: 30 minutes

Ingredient List:

- 2/3 cup of tapenade (capers, black olives, olive oil)
- 10 oz. of baby arugula
- ½ cup of goat cheese, soft
- 24 slices of bread, whole wheat, with crust removed
- Sea salt and black pepper, ground

Preparation:

1. Spread ½ of the bread slices with goat cheese and season them using salt ground pepper. Top with arugula greens.

2. Spread the other 12 slices with tapenade. Place that side down on top of the arugula. Halve the sandwiches diagonally and serve.

Recipe 21: Quintessential Egg Sandwich

This sandwich started when someone online took a photo of a typical egg sandwich. Those are so simple. The beauty of this sweet and savory sandwich is that you only need to follow several breakfast sandwich tips to find success.

Don't be afraid to use different varieties of bread - whether you use English muffins, bagels or toast, as long as it is substantial. Always fry the eggs in bacon fat. That's what Makes them so breakfast-y. Be sure to use more eggs than cheese. This isn't a grilled cheese sandwich. Include the jam. It sounds odd, but it gives this sandwich an essential sweet note, which balances the savory ingredients.

Yield: 2 Servings

Preparation Time: 20 minutes

Ingredient List:

- 4 tablespoons of jam, strawberry
- 2 slices of cheddar cheese, sharp

- 4 slices of sandwich bread, your fav type
- 4 eggs, large
- 4 slices of crispy bacon

Preparation:

1. Cook bacon in a medium pan on med-low heat. Make it as crispy as you like it. Transfer bacon to a plate lined with paper towels. Reserve 2 tablespoons of bacon grease and pour the rest out.

2. Crack eggs into pan. Raise to med. heat. Sprinkle the black pepper on top of the eggs. Fry the eggs until whites are cooked fully and yolks have just set.

3. Toast the bread. Promptly place cheese on a slice and spread jam on another slice. Arrange bacon on top of the cheese, with the eggs on top of the bacon.

4. Top sandwich with other bread slice. Serve.

Recipe 22: Spinach, Hummus 'N Tomato Sandwich

Choose your favorite flavor of hummus to add plant-based protein and quick flavor to your day. Adding spinach or lettuce and a ripe tomato offers a great flavor match, with all the benefits of superfoods. It's beneficial for your health and it tastes great.

Yield: 2 Servings

Preparation Time: 15 minutes

Ingredient List:
- ½ cup of baby spinach
- 3 slices of tomatoes
- 2 tablespoons of hummus
- 2 slices of bread, multi-grain
- 1/8 teaspoons of salt, kosher

Preparation:

1. Toast the bread if you prefer toasted. Spread some hummus on one slice. Top it with the tomato slices, then layer the tomato with spinach.

2. Sprinkle with salt. Place second slice on top of spinach. Serve.

Recipe 23: Meatball Sub Sandwich

Don't you just love an easy, quick meal once in a while – especially when you just got home from a long day at work? Meatball sub sandwiches are a super tasty way to get dinner prepared quickly. They also happen to be perfect when all you want is a mobile meal.

Yield: 4 Servings

Preparation Time: 25 minutes

Ingredient List:
- ¼ cup of cheese, Parmesan
- 24 meatballs, cooked
- 1 cup of marinara sauce
- 2 tablespoons of olive oil, extra virgin
- 6 hoagie rolls

Preparation:

1. Place the hoagie rolls on baking sheet with open face up. Lightly drizzle oil over their surface.

2. Place rolls in oven on 400F for about five minutes. Rolls should only be lightly toasted.

3. Remove from oven for a moment. Spread the marinara on both tops of buns. Add the meatballs. Drizzle just a little more of the marinara sauce on meatballs. Sprinkle Parmesan cheese on them.

4. Return hoagies to oven. Bake for about 10 more minutes. The meatballs should be heated all the way through.

5. Serve. Have extra marinara sauce on the table, in case people want to dip.

Recipe 24: Spider Sandwich

OK, so this doesn't SOUND like a delicious sandwich choice, but read on. All you need for this recipe is a cookie cutter or drinking glass, mini chocolate chips, PBJ and pretzels. Your kids will enjoy helping with this one. If they don't like PBJ, you can use any other filling they prefer. If people in your house have peanut allergies, you can use something else for the spread.

Yield: 2 Servings

Preparation Time: 10 minutes

Ingredient List:

- 4 mini morsels, chocolate
- 8 pretzel sticks
- 2 tablespoons of jelly
- 2 tablespoons of peanut butter, creamy
- 2 slices of bread, your fav

Preparation:

1. Use a drinking glass or circular cookie cutter to cut two circles from bread slice. If you have a large-sized cookie cutter, you may need extra bread slices.

2. Spread creamy peanut butter on a circle and jelly on the other side. Put the circles together, forming the sandwich.

3. Break the pretzel sticks into two halves. Stick them between slices of bread.

4. Place the chocolate mini morsels on the top. They are the "eyes". Serve to your young sandwich-lovers.

Recipe 25: Turkey, Cream Cheese 'N Cranberry Sandwich

This recipe also harkens back to the day after Thanksgiving. I mean, before it was the biggest shopping day of the year, it was the best leftover day of the year. This turkey, cream cheese and cranberry sandwich helps leftovers to step up. No need to loosen that belt – this is not a heavy meal. The cream cheese goes so well with cranberries, and adding the greens Makes it a lovely and drool-worthy sandwich. It's perfect for informal lunches at work or even a midnight snack.

Yield: 4 Servings

Preparation Time: 20 minutes

Ingredient List:
- 2 slices of sandwich thins
- Mixed fresh salad greens
- 1 oz. of cranberry jelly

- 1 oz. of softened cream cheese, light
- 2 slices of cold roast turkey

Preparation:

1. Lightly toast the bread. Spread cream cheese on both sides. Mix cream cheese and cranberry jelly. If you prefer, you can use fresh or frozen cranberries, but canned jelly provides the smoothest texture.

2. Add greens and turkey. Split the sandwich in half. Serve.

Chapter Iii - Dessert Sandwiches

Recipe 26: Banana Fluff Sandwich

You'll be glad you found this recipe when you have a finicky child who doesn't like to eat fruit. This is a simple sandwich that is made with bananas and marshmallow fluff. It sounds weird, but it tastes great.

Yield: 1 Serving

Preparation Time: 15 minutes

Ingredient List:

- ½ sliced banana
- 2 tablespoons of marshmallow fluff
- 2 tablespoons of room temp. butter
- 2 slices of bread, wheat or white

Preparation:

1. Spread one side of bread pieces with butter. Spread marshmallow fluff on sides without butter. Layer using sliced bananas and close sandwiches. Serve.

Recipe 27: Monkey Toast Sandwich

The monkey toast sandwich features bananas, Nutella and peanut butter. Some people refer to it as a Snickers-toasty. White bread Makes it a favorite for the youngsters. When you spread the peanut butter on and pop the sandwich in a skillet, you will discover a sandwich that really does taste like a Snickers bar. It's a bit of a guilty pleasure, but hey, you deserve it after a long day at work.

Yield: 4 Servings

Preparation Time: 15 minutes

Ingredient List:

- 1 sliced medium banana
- 4 raisins, sliced
- White, wheat or cinnamon bread
- ¼ cup of peanut butter, creamy

Preparation:

1. Spread peanut butter evenly on two slices of bread. Top with the banana and the remainder of slices of bread.

2. Spray large skillet with cooking spray. Cook sandwiches in pan on med. heat until they are light brown. Turn once while cooking. Serve warm.

Recipe 28: Cream Cheese Berry Sandwich

Cream cheese and berry sandwiches are so easy to make. They only have a few ingredients, and none of them are so exotic that you can't find them at your local grocery store. The cream cheese, sweet berries and honey drizzle are sublime. The sweetness comes from your berries (they can be blueberries, blackberries, raspberries, etc.) and the creaminess comes from, of course, the cream cheese.

Yield: 2 Servings

Preparation Time: 15 minutes

Ingredient List:

- 4 slices of bread, country
- ¼ cup of cream cheese, softened
- 1 tablespoon of honey, pure
- ½ cup of berries, mixed

Preparation:

1. Place dry pan on stove top on med. heat.

2. Spread cream cheese on slices of bread. Top with berries. Drizzle with pure honey, making two sandwiches.

3. Cook in pan 'til heated through, golden brown and crisp. Serve hot.

Recipe 29: Granola Apple-Wich

If you are tired of attending parties where the dishes all have gluten, meat or dairy foods, make this apple-wich at home for your own party, or dessert for your family. These pseudo-sandwiches are made from raisins, oats, peanut butter and sliced apples. The apples will help to satisfy those rumblings in your stomach. They are easy to make and a healthy eating choice. You can enjoy them at any time of day. The peanut butter brings all the tastes together.

Yield: 5 Servings

Preparation Time: 25 minutes

Ingredient List:

- 2 tablespoons of raisins
- 5 tablespoons of granola
- 1 apple, cored, cut into ¼" thick rings.
- 10 tablespoons of peanut butter, creamy

Preparation:

1. Spread 2 tablespoons of peanut butter on ½ of apple rings. Sprinkle each one with 1 tablespoon of granola and several sandwiches.

2. Cover both with one apple ring each, forming apple sandwiches. Serve.

Recipe 30: Easy Ice Cream Sandwich

These ingenious ice cream sandwiches are a wonderful treat during the summer months. The thin cake bakes quite rapidly, so you won't have to have the oven on all day when the weather is hot. You don't even have to use any home-made filling ingredients. Allow the cake lots of time to freeze hard before you cut or wrap the sandwiches. The completed sandwiches should be frozen well before you serve them.

Yield: 12 Servings

Preparation Time: 55 minutes

Ingredient List:

- 2 pints of vanilla ice cream, high quality
- 2 teaspoons of vanilla extract, pure
- 2 eggs, large
- 1 cup of sugar, granulated
- 1 cup of flour, all-purpose
- 1 ½ sticks of butter, unsalted – melted and cooled + additional for greasing pan

- 3/4 teaspoons of baking powder
- 3/4 cup of cocoa powder
- 3/4 teaspoons of salt, coarse

Preparation:

1. Preheat the oven to 350F. Butter 18x13" rimmed cookie sheet. Use parchment paper to line it.

2. Whisk together salt, baking powder, cocoa powder and flour in medium bowl.

3. Whisk sugar and butter together in large bowl. Add the eggs, then beat it until it's smooth. Then beat in the vanilla. Add flour mixture. Beat 'til fully combined. Batter should become thick.

4. Scrape batter into pan. Smooth to even, thin layer. Leave a small parchment paper border around edges.

5. Bake mixture until the cake sets, or 10-12 minutes. Transfer cake to rack to completely cool.

6. When ready to assemble, take the ice cream out of the freezer. Allow it to sit for several minutes. It should become slightly softer.

7. Use parchment paper to transfer cake to floured cutting board. Cut it in half crossways so you have two 13x9" pieces.

8. Use a large-sized ice cream scoop to place ice cream over top of ½ of cake. Spread until even and flat. Place other ½ of cake on top of ice cream, top facing down. This Makes a large sized sandwich cake. Wrap it

promptly in cling wrap. Freeze for eight hours or more, until it is firm.

9. Remove large sandwich cake from freezer. Remove cling wrap. Trim ¼ inch from each edge. Cut into 12 small sandwiches.

10. Wrap each individual-sized ice cream sandwich in cling wrap. Freeze until they are firm. Serve whenever you prefer.

Pulled Pork And Kale Biscuit Sandwiches

DIRECTIONS

In the bowl of a slow cooker combine 1 tablespoon salt, 1 teaspoon pepper, brown sugar, and paprika. Spread the mixture evenly all over the pork. Add vinegar, chicken stock, 1/4 cup ketchup, 3 crushed garlic cloves, onions, and 1 cup water. Cook on low for 8 hours.

Remove pork from braising liquid and shred using two forks in a mixing bowl. Strain liquid and transfer to a sauce pan with the remaining ketchup. Bring to a boil and simmer until it's been reduced by half. Add the sauce to the shredded pork.

Meanwhile, bake biscuits according to package instructions. In a large skillet over medium-high heat add 1 tablespoon olive oil and 1 garlic clove, thinly sliced; sauté for 1 minute. Add kale and chicken stock; season with salt and black pepper. Stir-fry until the kale has wilted. Drain the excess liquid and transfer to a bowl.

Assemble sandwiches by splitting biscuits, topping with garlicky kale, a mound of pulled pork, and garnish with pickled jalapeños. Serve immediately.

INGREDIENTS

- Kosher salt
- Freshly ground black pepper
- 1/2 c. brown sugar
- 2 tsp. paprika
- 2 lb. boneless pork shoulder, trimmed of excess fat

- 1/4 c. vinegar
- 2 c. chicken stock
- 1/2 c. ketchup
- 4 garlic cloves
- 2 onions, cut in half
- 1 pkg. refrigerated biscuit dough
- 1 large head of kale, chopped into 1" to 2" pieces
- 1 garlic clove, thinly sliced
- 1/4 c. chicken stock
- Jar sliced jalapeños, for garnish

Chicken Parm Sliders

DIRECTIONS

Bake chicken nuggets according to package instructions. If using tenders, cut into slider size once baked.

Place a layer of potato roll bottoms on a parchment-lined baking sheet. Spoon over half the marinara and top with chicken nugget. Place mozzarella slices on top, completely covering layer of chicken nuggets. Spoon more marinara over cheese.

Top with bun tops and brush with melted butter. Sprinkle with Parmesan and parsley and bake until cheese is melty and sliders warmed through, 10 minutes.

INGREDIENTS

- 10 frozen chicken nuggets or tenders
- 10 slider potato rolls or buns
- 1/2 c. marinara
- 6 slices mozzarella
- 2 tbsp. grated Parmesan
- 2 tbsp. chopped fresh parsley

Slow-Cooker French Dip

DIRECTIONS

In a slow-cooker, combine 3 pounds beef chuck roast, 2 cups low-sodium beef broth, 1/4 cup soy sauce, 1 thinly sliced onion, 4 cloves chopped garlic, 2 tablespoons Worcestershire, 1 tablespoon fresh rosemary and 1 tablespoon fresh thyme and season with pepper.

Cover and cook on high until beef is tender, 5 to 6 hours.

Transfer beef to a cutting board and thinly slice. Skim fat of jus (save for dipping!).

Make sandwiches: Preheat oven to 350 degrees F. Top hoagies with meat and top with provolone and parsley. Brush rolls with melted butter and bake until cheese is melty, 5 minutes.

Serve sandwiches au jus.

INGREDIENTS
- 3 beef chuck roast
- 1 c. low-sodium beef broth
- 1 c. water
- 1/4 c. low-sodium soy sauce
- 1 large onion, thinly sliced
- 4 cloves garlic, chopped
- 2 tbsp. Worcestershire
- 4 Fresh rosemary sprigs
- 4 fresh thyme sprigs
- Freshly ground black pepper

FOR SANDWICHES
- hoagie rolls
- sliced provolone
- chopped fresh parsley
- Melted butter, for brushing rolls

Egg In A Hole Breakfast Sandwich

DIRECTIONS

Fry bacon over medium heat until crispy. Drain bacon and wipe skillet clean.

Using a small glass or biscuit cutter, cut a hole into one slice of bread.

Return skillet to medium heat. Add butter and toast both slices of bread.

Flip when golden and crack the egg into the hole. Season to taste with salt and pepper. Add avocado slices, cheese and bacon to the other slice of bread. Cover the skillet and cook until the egg whites are cooked through and the cheese is melted, about 3 minutes.

INGREDIENTS
- 2 slices bacon
- 2 slices cheddar
- 1/2 avocado, thinly sliced
- 1 eg
- 1 tbsp. butter
- kosher salt
- Freshly ground black pepper

Chicken Parm Sub

DIRECTIONS

Preheat oven to 350 degrees F. Prepare breading station with 3 large mixing bowls: one with breadcrumbs and parmesan cheese mixed together, another with eggs beaten with 1 tablespoon water, and the last with flour. Season chicken with salt and pepper. Coat each piece of chicken in flour and shake off excess, then dip into egg and coat in breadcrumbs. Repeat steps for remaining chicken and set aside on a plate.

In a large cast iron skillet add 1" oil over medium-high heat. When pan is hot but not smoking add chicken cutlets. Cook until golden brown, about 1 to 2 minutes on each side. Transfer to a paper towel–lined plate.

In a small sauce pan, warm up tomato sauce.

Meanwhile, in a rimmed sheet pan lined with parchment paper, place hero rolls cut-side up. Toast until lightly golden brown, about 1 to 2 minutes. Place chicken cutlets on bottom halves of hero rolls and top with sliced mozzarella cheese. Toast again until cheese begins to melt. Add spoonfuls of warm tomato sauce and 3 or 4 fresh basil leaves between the chicken and hero rolls. Close sandwich and cut in half. Serve immediately.

INGREDIENTS
- 2 c. panko breadcrumbs
- 2 large eggs

- 2 c. all-purpose flour
- 1 1/2 lb. chicken cutlets, cut in half lengthwise
- kosher salt
- Freshly ground black pepper
- canola oil
- 1 lb. fresh mozzarella, sliced 1/4" thick
- 4 hero rolls, cut in half lengthwise
- 2 c. tomato sauce
- Fresh basil

Chimichurri Steak Sandwich

DIRECTIONS

In the bowl of a food processor add cilantro, 1/2 cup basil, red onion, garlic, 1 teaspoon salt, red pepper flakes, and vinegar. Pulse a few times and scrape down sides of the bowl. While motor is running, drizzle in olive oil and process until almost smooth, but leave some texture. Set aside.

Preheat grill on medium-high heat. Drizzle steak with olive oil and season with salt and pepper. Place on grill and cook until lightly charred, about 3 minutes on each side. Transfer to a clean plate and loosely tent with foil; let the meat rest.

Meanwhile, toast bread on grill until slightly charred. Slice steak thinly on diagonal against the grain.

Spread chimichurri on toasted bread. Layer sliced steak with tomatoes and a few basil leaves. Top with toasted bread to close the sandwich.

INGREDIENTS
- 1/2 c. fresh cilantro
- 3/4 c. fresh basail
- 1/2 c. Chopped red onion
- 3 garlic cloves, chopped
- kosher salt
- 1/2 tsp. crushed red pepper flakes
- 3 tbsp. red wine vinegar
- extra-virgin olive oil

- 1 lb. skirt steak
- Freshly ground black pepper
- 1 loaf country bread, sliced 1/2" thick
- 2 large heirloom tomatoes, sliced 1/4" thick

Grilled Cheese With Tomatoes And Bacon

DIRECTIONS

Season tomatoes with sea salt and Set aside.

Preheat large cast iron skillet over medium-high heat. Place bacon in an even layer and cook until crisp, about 1 minute per side. Transfer to a paper towel–lined plate.

Spread each piece of bread with a thin layer of mayonnaise. Reduce heat to medium. Place bread in cast iron skillet mayonnaise-side down. Top with layers of gruyere on one half of the bread and provolone on other side. Placed sliced tomatoes and bacon on one side of bread. Cover skillet.

When cheese has begun to melt, top the tomatoes and bacon with another bread slice, mayonnaise-side up. Flip occasionally until both sides are golden brown. Serve immediately.

INGREDIENTS
- 2 large heirloom tomatoes, sliced 1/4" thick
- sea salt, such as Maldon
- 12 oz. bacon
- 1/2 c. mayonnaise
- 8 slices Pullman bread, cut 1/2" thick
- 1/2 lb. sliced gruyere cheese
- 1/2 lb. sliced provolone

Italian Club

DIRECTIONS

Place tomatoes on a paper towel–lined cutting board and sprinkle with sea salt. Set aside.

Preheat large cast iron skillet over medium-high heat. Place bacon in an even layer and cook until crisp, about 1 minute per side. Transfer to a paper towel–lined plate.

Place toast on a cutting board and spread with a layer of mayonnaise. Top with alternating layers of mortadella, spinach, bacon, tomatoes, and cheese. Top with toast and spread with a layer of pesto with alternating layers of ham, artichoke hearts, salami, and spinach. Spread the last pieces of toast with mayonnaise and place on top. Garnish with sliced pickles and secure sandwich with toothpicks.

INGREDIENTS

- 2 large heirloom tomatoes, sliced 1/4" thick
- sea salt, such as Maldon
- 8 slices bacon
- 12 slices 1/2" thick Pullman bread, toasted
- 1/2 c. mayonnaise
- 1/4 lb. thinly sliced mortadella
- 2 c. spinach
- 1/2 lb. thinly sliced provolone
- 1/2 c. pesto
- 1/4 lb. thinly sliced ham

- 4 marinated artichoke hearts, sliced in half lengthwise
- 1/2 lb. thinly sliced Genoa salami
- sweet pickles
- Toothpicks

Hash Brown Breakfast Sandwiches

DIRECTIONS

Pour the hash browns onto a large paper towel or clean dish towel, wrapping them up and squeezing them to drain out any excess water. Pour the dried hash browns into a medium-sized mixing bowl. Add 2 eggs, garlic powder, salt, and pepper and mix to combine.

Over medium heat, spray a skillet with cooking spray (or spread with butter). Place the twist-top from a large mason jar (or a large biscuit cutter or circular cookie cutter) in the skillet. Spoon the hash brown mixture into the mason jar lid, mashing it down a bit to form a patty. Let cook until a golden crust forms along the bottom, about 2 to 3 minutes. Use tongs to remove the mason jar lid, and use a spatula to flip the hash brown patty. Repeat until you've made 8 patties. (You can keep them warm in the oven at 200 degrees F while you cook the rest.)

Over medium heat, using the same skillet and mason jar lid, crack an egg into the center of the lid. (Some of the egg may pour out, but this will help keep it generally the same size/shape as the hash brown patties.) Cook until the white has set and the yolk is still a little runny, about 3 to 4 minutes. Use tongs to remove the mason jar lid, and set aside the cooked egg. Repeat with remaining eggs.

As the eggs cook, cook the bacon in a separate pan over medium heat, cooking until the fat has turned translucent white and the bacon has curled up a bit. Set strips on a paper towel–lined plate to drain excess grease.

Place a slice of cheddar cheese on four of the hash brown patties. Top each with an egg, Sriracha, and two bacon slices. Cover with another hash brown patty, making four sandwiches total.

INGREDIENTS
- 1 bag frozen hash browns (10 oz.), thawed
- 6 eggs
- 1 tbsp. garlic powder
- 1/2 tsp. garlic powder
- 1/2 tsp. kosher salt
- 1/2 tsp. Freshly ground black pepper
- 4 strips thick-cut bacon, cut in half
- 4 slices sharp cheddar
- Sriracha, to taste

Sriracha Meatloaf

DIRECTIONS

Preheat oven to 375 degrees F. Line a sheet pan with parchment paper and set aside. In a small bowl mix together ketchup and Sriracha. Divide mixture into 2 bowls containing 3/4 cup and 1/2 cup.

In the bowl of a food processor add onion, carrot, celery, parsley, and garlic. Pulse until combined, then transfer into a large mixing bowl. Add 2 teaspoons salt, 1 teaspoon pepper, panko, and egg; mix with a spoon or by hand. Add meat and 1/2 cup Sriracha ketchup; mix by hand until just incorporated.

Divide meatloaf into 4 equal parts. Shape each in to a rectangle about 1" high; place on parchment paper. Spread 1 tablespoon ketchup on each piece using back of a spoon or a brush. Bake for 20 minutes.

Assemble sandwiches by layering lettuce, tomato, red onion, and meatloaf between 2 pieces of bread. Serve with remaining 1/2 cup Sriracha ketchup.

INGREDIENTS
- 1 1/4 c. ketchup
- 1/4 c. sriracha
- 1/2 c. chopped onion
- 1/2 c. chopped carrots
- 1/2 c. chopped celery
- 3/4 c. chopped parsley
- 2 garlic cloves, roughly chopped
- kosher salt

- Freshly ground black pepper
- 3/4 c. panko (Japanese bread crumbs)
- 1 egg, beaten
- 1 lb. ground beef
- 1 lb. ground pork
- 4–6 pieces greenleaf lettuce
- 1 large beefsteak tomato, sliced
- 1 large red onion, sliced
- 8 slices crusty country bread

Chicken And Waffles Breakfast Sandwich

DIRECTIONS

Place chicken in 1 cup buttermilk and allow to marinate overnight

Prepare dredge for chicken by combining 1 cup flour with 2 tsp. salt and cayenne. Remove chicken from buttermilk and coat in flour mixture. Place chicken back in buttermilk and then back into flour for second coating. Heat oil to 350 degrees F and fry chicken for 5 to 7 minutes or until internal temperature of 165 degrees F is reached. Set aside.

To make waffles, combine 1 cup flour, sugar, baking powder, baking soda, and 1/4 tsp. salt in large bowl and whisk together. In separate bowl combine 1 lightly beaten egg, 1 cup buttermilk, and 1/4 cup melted butter. Pour wet ingredients into dry ingredients and whisk together to form batter. Pour about 1/3 cup (exact amount will depend on your waffle iron) batter onto waffle iron and cook for 3 to 4 minutes until golden brown and crisp*.

Melt butter in pan over medium-low heat and crack in remaining egg. Fry until white is set and yolk is still runny. In small bowl, combine honey and hot sauce.

To build sandwich, place chicken on waffle and drizzle with hot sauce mixture. Top with fried egg and another waffle.

INGREDIENTS

- 1 chicken breast, pounded out to an even thickness

- 2 c. buttermilk
- 2 c. all-purpose flour
- 2 tsp. + 1/4 tsp. Kosher salt
- 1 tsp. cayenne
- Vegetable oil, for frying
- 1 tbsp. sugar
- 1 tsp. baking powder
- 1/2 tsp. baking soda
- 2 eggs, divided
- 1/4 c. + 1/2 tbsp. butter, melted
- 1 tbsp. honey
- 1 tbsp. Hot sauce

Egg In A Hole Blt

DIRECTIONS

Fry bacon over medium-high heat (starting with bacon on cold pan) until desired level of crispness is achieved.

Using small glass, cut hole in center of one piece of bread. Melt butter in large pan over medium-low heat and add both pieces of bread. Toast on one side for 2 minutes and then flip. Crack egg into hole and lower heat. Continue to cook low and slow until white is set, about 5 minutes. Remove intact piece of bread when second side is lightly toasted.

Spread mayo on intact piece of bread and top with tomato, lettuce, and bacon. Place on second piece bread and slice sandwich in half on an angle through the yolk.

INGREDIENTS
- 4 slices of bacon
- 1 tbsp. butter
- 2 slices of bread
- 1 egg
- 1/2 tbsp. mayo
- tomato, sliced
- Iceberg lettuce, torn

Breakfast Burger

DIRECTIONS

Form beef into ball and flatten into burger shaped patty. Using small glass, cut out center of the patty to form a donut shaped burger. Season with salt and pepper.

Preheat cast-iron skillet to medium high heat and melt in 1 tbsp. butter. Place burger seasoned side down and season the other side. Cook for 2 minutes on first side then flip. After the flip, crack egg into center of burger. Cover pan with lid and cook until white has set. When burger is done, immediately top with cheese so it will melt.

Melt remaining butter in separate pan over medium high heat and add in shredded hashbrowns. Fry until golden brown and crispy.

Place bun, cut side down, in pan used to cook burgers. Toast until lightly browned.

To build burger, spread ketchup on bottom bun then place burger on top. Top burger with hashbrowns and top bun. Slice burger in half to reveal egg inside.

INGREDIENTS

- 1/3 lb. ground chuck (per burger)
- kosher salt
- Black pepper
- 2 tbsp. butter, divided
- 1 egg

- 1 slice cheddar cheese
- 1/2 c. shredded hashbrowns
- 1 tbsp. ketchup
- Burger bun

Steak and Egg Breakfast Sandwich

DIRECTIONS

Remove steak from fridge and allow it to come to room temperature (30 minutes). Generously season both sides with salt and pepper. Grill on high for 2 to 3 minutes per side. Allow steak to rest for at least 5 minutes then thinly slice it against the grain.

To make chimichurri, combine parsley, cilantro, garlic, red wine vinegar, and olive oil in food processor. Pulse until combined and season with salt and pepper.

Slice ciabatta bun in half and toast until lightly browned.

Melt butter in pan over medium-low heat and crack in egg. Fry until white is set and yolk is still runny.

To build sandwich, place sliced steak on bottom bun and drizzle with chimichurri. Top with fried egg and more chimichurri if desired. Place top half of ciabatta on top of egg.

INGREDIENTS

- 1 steak (1-in. thick)
- kosher salt
- Black pepper
- 1/2 c. Parsley

- 1/4 c. cilantro
- 1 clove garlic
- 3 tbsp. red wine vinegar
- 1/3 c. extra-virgin olive oil
- 1 ciabatta bun
- 1/2 tbsp. butter
- 1 egg

Chicken Meatball Sliders With Mozzarella And Wilted Spinach

DIRECTIONS

Preheat oven to 450 degrees F and oil a small metal baking dish.

In medium bowl, using your hands, combine chicken, egg, garlic, salt, pepper, fennel seeds, crushed red pepper flakes, breadcrumbs, and parsley until combined.

Divide mixture into 8 meatballs (use an ice cream scoop for a perfect shape) and place close together in baking dish. Bake 12 minutes.

Pour sauce over meatballs, then return to oven for 3 minutes more, until sauce is heated through, and meatballs register an internal temperature of 165 degrees F. Heat broiler.

Heat remaining 1 tablespoon olive oil in a large skillet. Sauté spinach until just-wilted, 2 minutes. Season with lemon juice and salt and pepper.

Top each meatball with mozzarella and place under broiler 1 to 2 minutes, until cheese is melted and bubbling.

Make sliders by topping meatballs on buns and topping with sautéed spinach.

INGREDIENTS

- 2 tbsp. extra-virgin olive oil

- 1 lb. ground chicken
- 1 egg
- 1 Garlic clove, minced
- Sea salt
- Freshly ground pepper
- 1/2 tsp. fennel seeds, ground
- 1/2 tsp. red pepper flakes
- 1/2 c. panko breadcrumbs
- 1/4 c. finely chopped parsley
- 2 c. good-quality marinara sauce
- 12 oz. baby spinach
- Juice of 1/2 lemon
- 8 slices mozzarella (from 8 oz. ball)
- 8 slider buns, heated

Open-Faced Bacon Avocado Tomato Sandwich

DIRECTIONS

In a large skillet, fry bacon over medium heat until brown and crisp, about 8 minutes. Transfer to a paper towel-lined plate.

In a medium bowl, combine avocados, lemon juice, and red pepper flakes. Season with salt and pepper.

Spread each slice of toasted bread with avocado and top with 2 tomato slices. Season with salt and pepper and top with bacon.

INGREDIENTS
- 8 slices bacon
- 2 ripe avocados, mashed
- 2 tbsp. lemon juice
- 1/2 tsp. crushed red pepper flakes
- kosher salt
- Black pepper
- 8 slices whole-grain bread, toastd
- 3 large heirloom tomatoes, sliced

Bonus: Lemony Crab Rolls

DIRECTIONS

In medium bowl, whisk together mayonnaise, lemon zest and juice, Old Bay, green onions, salt and pepper. Gently fold in crab meat until just combined.

Heat large nonstick skillet over medium-high heat. Brush sides of buns with melted butter and cook until golden, about 2 minutes per side.

Line each roll with 1 leaf Bibb lettuce and spoon in crab mixture. Sprinkle with Old Bay seasoning and serve with lemon wedges.

INGREDIENTS
- 1/2 c. mayonnaise
- 2 tsp. lemon zest
- 2 tbsp. lemon juice
- 1 1/2 tsp. Old Bay seasoning, plus more for garnish
- 1/4 c. green onions, thinly sliced
- kosher salt
- Freshly ground black pepper
- 1 lb. pound lump crab meat
- 4 top-split buns
- 2 tbsp. butter, melted
- 4 leaves Bibb lettuce
- Lemon wedges, for serving

Part 2

Chapter 1: Abc Sandwich

1 cup mayonnaise

1/2 cup minced scallions

2 tablespoons brandy

1/4 teaspoon coarsely-ground black pepper

18 slices toasted whole-wheat bread

Leaf lettuce

12 ounces crabmeat, picked over well to remove any shells

Tomato slices

12 slices slab bacon, cut in half,

Cooked crisp and drained

2 avocados, sliced

Combine the mayonnaise, brandy and scallion, in a small bowl and mix very well. For each sandwich, place three pieces of bread with little of the mixed mayonnaise. Cover the first slice of bread with lettuce leaves, 2 ounces of crabmeat, and one or two tomato slices. Put the second slice of bread, a layer of avocado slices, and top with the four half-slices of bacon, one or two tomato slice, and more lettuce. Secure the sandwich with a wooden picks and cover with the third slice of bread, if you like, and slice it in half.

Serve the sandwiches immediately.

Acapulco Fishburgers

1 pound fish fillets

1 medium green bell pepper, chopped

3 medium onions, chopped

2 cups soft bread crumbs

3/4 teaspoon salt

1/4 teaspoon pepper

3 tablespoons shortening

Bone fish; put through food chopper or chop finely with knife. Combine with green pepper, onions, bread crumbs, salt and pepper; mix well. Create 8 different patties about 4 inches in diameter. Brown on two sides in a short skillet and allow moderate heat for 10 to 15 minutes.

Alaska Salmon Salad Sandwich

15 1/2 ounces canned Alaska salmon

1/3 cup plain nonfat yogurt

1/3 cup chopped green onions

1/3 cup chopped celery

1 tablespoon lemon juice

Black pepper, to taste

12 slices bread

Drain and flake salmon. Stir in remaining ingredients except pepper and bread. Season with pepper to taste. Place mixture of salmon on half of bread slice; close it up with remaining bread. Cut sandwiches into halves or quarters.

Make 6 sandwiches.

Asian Turkey Burgers

1 pound ground turkey

1 1/3 cups canned French fried onions, divided

1 egg

1/2 cup finely chopped water chestnuts

1/4 cup dry breadcrumbs

3 tablespoons teriyaki sauce

1 tablespoon Frank's RedHot sauce

2 teaspoons grated fresh ginger

4 sandwich buns

Shredded lettuce

Make combination of turkey, egg, 1 cup French fried onions, water chestnuts, breadcrumbs, teriyaki sauce, hot sauce and ginger. Shape into 4 patties. Cook about 6 inches over a medium from heat or grill, heat for about 10 minutes or until it no longer pinkish in center, then turn once.

Serve on buns, covered with the remaining 1/3 cup French fried onions and lettuce.

Chapter 2: Avocado Chicken Melt

4 boneless skinless chicken breast halves

1/2 cup cornmeal

1 teaspoon garlic salt

2 tablespoons vegetable oil

1/2 well ripe avocado, peeled and sliced thin and divided

1 cup shredded Monterey jack cheese

4 wheat bread slices, toasted

1/2 cup plain yogurt

1/4 cup chopped sweet red bell pepper

Wash chicken with cold water and use paper towel to pat dry it. Put it between two sheets of plastic wrap and pound to flatten to 1/4-inch thickness.

Combine cornmeal and garlic salt in a resealable bag. Put chicken; close bag and toss to coat well. In large nonstick frying pan, heat oil. Allow chicken for about 2 minutes to cook in hot oil until it is light brown. Remove chicken from nonstick frying pan and put in a shallow baking pan.

Place half of avocado slices on the chicken and sprinkle evenly with shredded cheese. Bake at 350 degrees F and make sure chicken is done and cheese is melted.

Put each of chicken breast on a slice of toast. Top with remaining avocado slices. In small bowl, combine pepper and yoghurt; serve with chicken.

Couzan Billy Burger

Well I did get to test a new burger a while back...just haven't posted it yet. It is fairly uniqueand combines some tastes you may not think work. Give it a try......

Cut thick slices of red onion...about 1/2 inch for you onion lovers...thinner for the rest of us!

Grill these over a low heat and use your favorite BBQ sauce to both sides. Be careful not to burn and over cook. Set these aside and cover loosely with foil. Then prepare your burger usually to taste and toast your buns. Put the onion slice on the bottom bun, then the burger and put on top your favorite bleu Cheese dressing. This topping can be homemade very easily. Here are a couple of ideas......

Mix bleu cheese with butter. Apply enough butter to prevent the cheese from crumbling.

Mix bleu cheese with Mayo or sour cream, add some salt and pepper and a few drops of Tabasco sauce. I mix mine with Miracle Whip and Tabasco...again just enough to prevent the cheese from crumbling. I do this in my little hand processor.

I will try to get more accurate measurements this weekend for the above bleu cheese dressings

Crescent Monte Cristo Loaf

2 (8 ounce) cans refrigerated crescent dinner rolls

2 tablespoons butter or margarine, melted

2 tablespoons honey

6 ounces thinly sliced smoked turkey

6 ounces thinly sliced Muenster cheese

6 ounces thinly sliced cooked ham

1/3 to 1/2 cup red raspberry preserves

Topping

2 tablespoons honey

1 tablespoon sesame seeds

Separate dough into 4 long rectangles. Put rectangles crosswise on 1 large or 2 small cookie sheets (rectangles should not touch), firmly press perforations to seal.

In small bowl, combine 2 tablespoons honey and butter, mix well. Brush over dough. Bake at 375 degrees F for 8 to 12 minutes or until golden brown; cool 15 minutes.

Put oil in a 15 x 10 x 1 inch baking pan. Carefully place one crust on pan. Top evenly with turkey.

Put second crust over turkey; cover with cheese and ham. Put third crust over ham; spread evenly with preserves. Cover with fourth crust; brush top with 2 tablespoons honey and sprinkle with sesame seeds.

Bake at 375 degrees F for 10 to 15 minutes or until loaf is deep golden brown. Let stand 5 minutes. Cut into 6 to 8 slices.

Chili Dog Rolls

-----ROLLS-----

1 tb Yeast, dry

1/4 c -- water, warm

1/2 ts Sugar or honey

1 c -- water, warm

1 tb Olive oil

4 c Flour, unbleached or whole wheat flour

-----FILLING-----

7/8 c -- water, boiling

1 c TVP® granules or flakes

1 md Onion -- chopped

1/2 Green pepper -- chopped

1 Garlic clove -- minced

1 c Mushrooms (6 large) -- chopped

2 ts Olive oil

1 tb Olive oil

1 t Cumin

2 ts Chili powder

1 t Oregano

1/2 ts Salt

1 lg Tomato -- chopped OR 8 oz Tomato sauce

Dissolve the yeast in 1/4 cup warm water and honey, and let stand a few minutes. Add 1 cup of warm water and 1 tbs olive oil. Stir in the flour.

Put the dough on a work surface and knead up to 5 minutes or more until it turn smooth, add more flour if need be. Cover and let rise for an hour.

For the filling: Mix the boiling water and TVP®. Let it stand while you prepare the vegetables. Add 2 tsp olive oil when you heat a non-stick skillet.

Sauté the onions, pepper and garlic a few minutes to soften, then remove to a bowl.

Add 1 Tbsp olive oil after heating the pan again. Sauté the reconstituted TVP® a minute or two, sprinkling with the spices. Cook a few minutes and add the tomato or tomato sauce. Divide into 2 balls after punching down the risen dough.

Have 2 lightly oiled baking dishes ready. On a lightly floured surface, roll a ball of dough out into a long oblong, about 5 inches wide. Spread half the filling down the long side of the dough, leaving edges bare.

Roll dough over to seal filling in, pinching edges.

Cut each roll of dough into 10 pieces, placing slices on baking sheets, seam side down. Let it rise again for 20 minutes. Heat oven to 375 degrees, and bake for 20-25 minutes until lightly browned. Cool on a rack.

Chapter 3: Baked Pizza Sandwich

Yield: 6 servings

1 lb Lean Ground Beef

15 oz Tomato Sauce; 1 Cn, OR

15 oz Pizza Sauce; 1 Cn

1 ts Oregano Leaves

2 c Biscuit Baking Mix

1 ea Egg; Lg

2/3 c Milk

8 oz Cheese; *

2 oz Mushrooms; Sliced, Drained, 1Cn

1/4 c Parmesan Cheese; Grated

* Use 1 8-oz package of sliced process mozzarella or American cheese.

Heat the oven to 400 degrees F.

Cook and stir the meat until it turn in a large skillet.

Drain off the excess fat. Stir in the oregano leaves and half of the tomato sauce into the meat mixture.

Heat till boiling, and then reduce the heat and simmer, uncovered, for 10 minutes. While the meat mixture is simmering, mix the baking mixture, egg and the milk.

Measure out 3/4 cup of the batter and set aside.

Spread the remaining batter in a greased baking pan, 9 X 9 X 2-inches. Spread evenly after pouring the remaining tomato sauce over the batter. Layer 4 slices of the cheese, the mushrooms, the meat mixture and the remaining cheese on top of the batter and tomato sauce. Put the reserved batter on the top of the cheese. Sprinkle the grated Parmesan cheese on top of the batter and bake uncovered, until it is golden brown, allow for 20 to 25 minutes. Cool it for 5 minutes before cutting into squares and serving.

All-American Barbecue Sandwiches

4 1/2 pounds Ground beef

1 1/2 cups Onion -- chopped

2 1/4 cups Catsup

3 tablespoons prepared mustard

3 tablespoons Worcestershire sauce

2 tablespoons Vinegar

2 tablespoons Sugar

1 tablespoon Salt

1 tablespoon Pepper

18 Hamburger buns -- split

In a Dutch oven, cook beef and onion until meat turn brown and onion is tender; drain. Combine catsup, mustard, Worcestershire, sugar, vinegar, salt and pepper; stir into beef mixture. Heat through. Serve on buns.

Fired Up Over Turkey Barbeque,"Grilled Crab Sandwich

1 cup crab meat, drained and flaked

1/2 cup shredded process American cheese

1/4 cup chopped celery

2 tablespoons sweet pickle relish, drained

2 tablespoons chopped green onions, with tops

1 hard cooked egg, chopped

3 tablespoons mayonnaise

1/2 teaspoon lemon juice

10 slices bread, buttered

5 large tomato slices

PREPARATION:

Combine crab meat, cheese, celery, relish, green onions, hard cooked egg, mayonnaise, and lemon juice. Spread on unbuttered side of 5 bread slices. Add a tomato slice to top of each sandwich then season with salt and pepper. Top with remaining bread slices, buttered side up.

Grill on a griddle, Panini maker, or skillet, until sandwiches are golden brown on both sides. Make 5 sandwiches.

Chapter 4: Texas Barbecue Sandwich

Ingredients:

2 cups GRILLED TURKEY

3/4 cup tomato juice

1/4 cup catsup

2-2/3 Tbsp vinegar

2 Tbsp molasses

1-1/2 Tbsp Worcestershire sauce

1 Tbsp each dried onions and sugar

2 tsp paprika

3/4 tsp each salt and dry mustard

1/2 tsp each chili powder, dried minced garlic and cayenne pepper- dash hot pepper sauce

4 hamburger buns, split horizontally and toasted

Servings: 4

Instructions:

1. Cut meat from bones and mince. 2. In 3-quart saucepan, over high heat, combine tomato juice, catsup, vinegar, molasses, Worcestershire sauce, onions, sugar, paprika, salt, dry mustard, chili powder, garlic, cayenne pepper and hot pepper sauce; bring to boil. Reduce heat and simmer 10 minutes. Add turkey

and simmer 10 to 15 minutes or until heated throughout. 3. To serve, spoon barbeque on bottom half of burger bun. Top with other half.

Italian Pork Sandwiches

Ingredients:

1 pound boneless pork, cut into 3/4-inch cubes

1 8-ounce bottle low-calorie Italian dressing (purchased)

4 French-style rolls, split and toasted

Servings: 4

Instructions:

In self-sealing plastic bag, marinate pork cubes in dressing, refrigerated, overnight (6-24 hours).

Discard dressing and thread pork cubes onto barbecue skewers. (Note: If using wooden skewers, soak skewers in water for an hour before using to prevent burning.) Grill or broil, about four inches from heat, for 8-10 minutes, turning to brown all sides. Place cubes inside rolls and serve with purchased marinated roasted peppers, if desired.

Submarine Sandwich

Italian delis are excellent for making terrific submarine sandwiches. But did you realize how incredibly easy they are to prepare at home? Using the best quality cold cuts and a great crusty loaf of Italian or French style bread, you too can make a satisfying meal in just minutes.

1/4 cup Italian vinaigrette

1 long crusty loaf (up to 16 inches) French or Italian bread

1/4 cup mayonnaise

2 small ripe tomatoes, thinly sliced

4 ounces prosciutto, thinly sliced

6 ounces Italian salami, thinly sliced

3 ounces cheddar cheese, thinly sliced

6 ounces boiled ham, thinly sliced

4 ounces provolone cheese, thinly sliced

12 slices dill pickles

1 cup shredded iceberg lettuce

12 small sweet pickled peppers, sliced.

Slice loaf of bread in half lengthwise and spread mayonnaise on both cut sides. Layer bottom half of loaf with tomato slices, salami, prosciutto, Cheddar, ham, provolone, and pickles. Top with lettuce and pickled peppers. Put vinaigrette over the filling and cover with top half. Press down firmly.

Serve 3 to 4.

Roasted Red Pepper Stuffed Sandwich

This stuffed sandwich is packed with flavor combining three cheeses, roasted red peppers, red onion and basil.

1 (1-pound) loaf Italian or French bread, cut in half lengthwise

1/2 cup prepared olive oil vinaigrette salad dressing

4 to 5 lettuce leaves

2 tomatoes, sliced 1/4-inch

6 slices (1/2-ounce each) LAND O LAKES® Chedarella®, Cheddar or Swiss Cheese

1/2 (7 1/4-ounce) jar (1/2 cup) roasted red pepper slices, drained

1/2 small red onion, thinly sliced

1/3 cup mild banana pepper rings

1/3 cup pitted ripe olives

6 to 8 fresh basil leaves*

Scoop out center of top half of bread, leaving behind 1/2-inch shell; set aside.

Brush both cut sides of bread with dressing. Layer bottom half of loaf with lettuce leaves, cheese, tomatoes, roasted red pepper, olives, banana pepper, onions and basil leaves. Cover with top half of bread. Wrap entire loaf in plastic food wrap. Refrigerate 1 hour before serving to blend flavors.

Remove from refrigerator 15 minutes before serving. Cut into slices.

Make 6 sandwiches.

*Substitute 1 teaspoon dried basil leaves.

Chapter 5: Palm Beach Sandwiches (A.K.A. Pimento Cheese Sandwiches)

Despite their genteel Floridian name, these cheddar-cheese- and-red-pepper-salad-filled sandwiches are popular throughout the South. Good cooks embellish them variously (substituting diced green chilies or homemade red pepper conserve for the roasted peppers or supplementing either with chopped pecans); hasty cooks don't hesitate to resort to jarred pimientos.

2 large heavy red sweet peppers

3/4 cup mayonnaise, fresh or purchased

1/2 cup thinly sliced green onions

1 tablespoon fresh lemon juice

1 tablespoon Dijon mustard

3/4 teaspoon hot pepper sauce

3/4 pound sharp Cheddar cheese, coarsely grated

16 thick slices white sandwich bread

Under a preheated broiler or in the flame of a gas burner, roast peppers, turning them, until the skins are lightly and evenly charred. Slip the peppers into a paper bag, cover the top and steam the peppers until cool. Remove the burnt peel, then stem and core the peppers and finely chop them.

In a large bowl, stir together the chopped peppers, green onions, mayonnaise, lemon juice, mustard, and hot pepper sauce. Gradually stir in the grated cheese, mixing thoroughly. The sandwich filling can be prepared about 1 day ahead. Cover and refrigerate; return it to room temperature before proceeding.

About 30 minutes before serving time, lay 8 slices of the bread on a work surface. Divide the filling equally among the slices, spreading it to the edges of the bread and using it all. Top with the remaining 8 slices of bread. With a serrated knife, carefully cut the sandwiches in half on the diagonal. Cover up sandwiches with plastic wrap and then drape them with a dampened towel until serving.

Serve 8.

Jumbo Party Sandwich

Thinly sliced roast beef, olives and provolone cheese are a sandwich classic—and a party favorite.

1 1/2 pounds thinly sliced cooked lean roast beef
1/2 cup sour cream
1 tablespoon horseradish-style mustard
1/4 teaspoon salt
1/8 teaspoon ground black pepper
1 round loaf white bread, unsliced (2 pounds)
1 clove garlic, minced
1/4 cup butter, softened
1 tablespoon snipped Italian parsley
1 teaspoon crushed dried basil
3 cups chopped lettuce
6 thin slices red onion, separated into rings
6 ounces fontinella or provolone cheese, sliced
1 red bell pepper, thinly sliced
1/4 cup sliced pitted ripe olives

Combine sour cream, mustard, salt and pepper; reserve.

Cut bread in half horizontally. Remove soft center of the bread, leaving about a 1-inch- thick shell.

Mash garlic; combine with butter, parsley and basil. Spread cut sides of bread with herb butter. To assemble, layer ingredients in the following order in bottom of loaf: lettuce, onion, cheese, roast beef, red pepper slices, sour cream dressing and olives. Cover with top of loaf. Cut into 8 wedges; serve immediately. Make 8 servings.

Ham Salad

A basic stand-by for leftover ham. Accompany with potato chips and sweet pickles.

3 cups coarsely ground ham

2 hard-cooked eggs, chopped

1/2 cup chopped celery

1/2 cup mayonnaise

1/4 cup diced sweet pickle

2 teaspoons prepared mustard

1/8 teaspoon black pepper

In medium bowl stir together all ingredients. Make about 3 3/4 cups, enough for 6 sandwiches.

Make sandwiches on whole wheat bread or soft sandwich buns, topped with lettuce leaves.

Make 6 servings.

Note: Have your butcher grind smoked ham for you, or grind leftover ham in a food processor or grinding attachment. One pound of ham will probably yield about 3 cups ground ham.

Ham And Cheese Party Loaf

This clever French loaf is packed with a savory ham salad and cubes of Swiss and cheddar cheese. Make ahead of time and keep well-wrapped in the refrigerator before slicing thinly to serve.

1 1/2 pounds fully cooked ham, ground fine

10 tablespoons butter, softened

3 tablespoons Dijon-style mustard

1/2 teaspoon ground allspice

1/8 teaspoon ground nutmeg

1/4 teaspoon ground black pepper

1/4 teaspoon dried thyme, crushed

1 1/2 ounces Swiss cheese, in one piece

1 1/2 ounces sharp Cheddar cheese, in one piece

1 long slender loaf French bread, up to 12 ounces

12 gherkins

In large bowl combine butter, allspice, mustard, nutmeg, pepper and thyme; mix until smooth. Add ground ham to butter mixture; blending well.

Slice cheddar cheese and Swiss cheese into 1/4-inch thick sticks.

Turn bread top side down; cut off ends. Make a lengthwise cut down the center of the loaf from one end to the other, and be careful not to cut through top side. Spread the bread apart carefully; hollow it out, leaving about 1/2-inch thick shell. (The bread cut out from the center can be dried and used for breadcrumbs).

Press half the ham mixture into the bread. Arrange the Swiss cheese sticks lengthwise in one row; arrange the gherkins as the center row, the cheddar as the third row. Press the remaining ham mixture on top. Wrap tightly in plastic wrap; then in foil. Refrigerate for several hours or overnight.

To serve, slice filled loaf thinly; arrange slices, overlapping, on the serving tray.

Make about 30 servings.

German-Style Ham Sandwich

6 slices (6 ounces) Black Forest or Westphalian ham, thinly sliced

1/4 cup apple butter*

1 tablespoon stone-ground mustard

2 Kaiser Rolls split

4 ounces sliced Emmental or other Swiss cheese

1 small cucumber, very thinly sliced

Bibb or Boston lettuce leaves

In a small bowl, stir together apple butter and mustard. Spread apple butter mixture on the cut surfaces of Kaiser Rolls. Fill Kaiser Rolls with ham, Emmental cheese, lettuce leaves and cucumber slices.

Serve 2.

*May substitute with mango chutney

Chapter 6: Egg Salad Spread Supreme

6 hard-cooked eggs, chopped

1/4 cup shredded zucchini

1/4 cup shredded carrots

2 tablespoons chopped celery

1 tablespoon chopped green onion

1/4 cup fat-free cream cheese, softened

2 tablespoons plain yogurt (or mayonnaise)

1/4 teaspoon seasoning salt

1/4 teaspoon dill weeds

Pinch of dry mustard, salt, and pepper

Combine eggs, carrots, zucchini, celery, and green onion in bowl; set aside.

Mix mayonnaise, cream cheese, and seasonings until thoroughly blended.

Combine cream cheese mixture and egg mixture. Cover and refrigerate until ready to use.

Make 6 servings.

Creamy Chicken And Braeburn Apple Sandwiches

1/2 cup mayonnaise

2 1/4 teaspoons lemon juice

1 teaspoon grated fresh gingerroot

1 cup cooked chicken, cut into 1/2-inch chunks

1 braeburn apple, cut into 1/2-inch chunks

1 celery rib, chopped

1 baguette

1 bunch watercress, basil or other herb

1 medium red onion, peeled and thinly sliced

In medium bowl, mix lemon juice, mayonnaise and ginger until thoroughly blended. Stir in chicken, apple and celery. Season with salt.

Cut baguette crosswise into 4 pieces, about 4 inches long. Cut each piece lengthwise, about 3/4 of the way through. Line each sandwich with watercress or basil; top with a heaping 1/2 cup of salad. Top with onion and season with black pepper.

Make 4 servings.

Chutney-Turkey Salad on Focaccia

This can be used as appetizers or main meal.

1/2 cup finely chopped celery

1/3 cup CROSSE & BLACKWELL Hot Mango Chutney

3 tablespoons mayonnaise

1 teaspoon sesame seeds, toasted

2 cups chopped cooked turkey

1 package BUITONI® Italian Herbs and Cheese Focaccia Bread Mix, prepared in accordance to package directions.

2 tablespoons extra virgin olive oil

1 small zucchini, cut lengthwise into 8 (1/4-inch) slices

1 (7 ounce) jar roasted red bell peppers, dry and sliced

8 spinach leaves.

2 tablespoons prepared Caesar dressing

4 teaspoons Dijon mustard

PREHEAT oven to 350*F.

COMBINE celery, chutney, mayonnaise and sesame seeds in medium bowl. Add turkey; toss to coat.

CUT prepared bread in half horizontally. Brush olive oil on cut sides. Place bread in single layers on jelly-roll pan. Bake at 350*F for 12 minutes or until toasted. Spread 1/2 cup turkey salad over bottom half. Top with zucchini slices, roasted peppers and spinach; drizzle dressing over vegetables. Spread mustard on the top half of bread; place on top of sandwich. Cut into 12 slices.

Make 12 appetizer servings.

Chicken-Vegetable Salad Filling

3 cups chopped, cooked chicken breast

1 cup fresh bean sprouts

1 cup chopped celery

1/2 cup chopped green bell pepper

1/2 cup chopped onion

1/3 cup mayonnaise

3 tablespoons lemon juice

1/2 teaspoon freshly ground pepper

3/4 teaspoon dry mustard

1/2 teaspoon seasoned salt

Combine chicken, bean sprouts, celery, green pepper and onion in a bowl; toss gently.

Combine remaining ingredients; stir well. Add to chicken mixture; toss gently to mix.

Make 8 servings.

Nola Rib-Eye Sandwich

16 new or small red potatoes, quartered

Salt

1/2 cup melted butter

1/4 pound (1 stick) unsalted butter

1/2 cup Roasted Garlic Puree

Freshly ground white pepper to taste

Vegetable oil for deep frying

1 medium-sized red onion, sliced thinly and separated into rings

1/2 cup Crystal Hot Sauce or any hot sauce you may like.

1 cup bleached all-purpose flour

Essence to taste

4 rib-eye steaks (about 10 ounces)

2 tbsp olive oil

1/4 cup Worcestershire sauce

4 large hoagie buns (each about 6 inches long), toasted

2 tbsp olive oil

Directions

1. Put the potatoes in a large saucepan and cover with salted water. Bring to a boil, reduce the heat to moderate, and cook until fork tender, 8 to 10 minutes. Preheat over 375 degrees. Brush each hoagie with butter and toast, 6 to 8 minutes. Remove potatoes

from heat and drain. Put the potatoes back in the pot over low heat to dry them, then mash with a potato masher. Add the heavy cream, butter, garlic puree and mix well, but remember the potatoes should be slightly lumpy. Season with salt and pepper. Set aside and keep warm.

2. In a large, heavy, deep pot or an electric fryer, heat 4 inches of vegetable oil to 360 degrees.

3. In a small mixing bowl, toss the onion with the hot sauce. Pour the flour in a shallow bowl and season with Essence. Dredge the onion rings in the flour, shaking them to remove excess flour.

Fry them in batches in the hot oil, turning them once, until it turn golden brown, 2 to 3 minutes. Drain on paper towels, and then season with Essence. Set aside and keep warm.

4. Rub the rib-eyes with the olive oil and season with Essence. Heat a large sauté pan over medium-high heat. Add the steaks and cook for 6 to 8 minutes on each side for medium-rare, 130 degrees to 140 degrees; 10 minutes for medium, 145 degrees to 150 degrees; 12 minutes for proper done, 155 degrees to 165 degrees. Remove the steaks from the sauté pan and add the Worcestershire, stirring to loosen any browned bits on the bottom of the pan.

Garlic Meatball Po'boys

Ingredients

1/2 pound of ground veal

1/2 pound of ground beef chuck

1/2 pound of ground pork

1/2 cup finely chopped yellow onion

1/2 teaspoon finely chopped garlic

1/4 cup finely chopped green onions or scallions (green part only)

1 large egg

1/4 cup fine dried bread crumbs

1 tablespoon Worcestershire sauce

1 1/2 teaspoons salt

3/4 tablespoon cayenne pepper

16 small cloves garlic, peeled

1/4 cup bleached all-purpose flour

1 teaspoon Creole Seasoning

1/4 cup vegetable oil

2 cups thinly sliced yellow onions

One 12-ounce bottle amber beer

1 cup water

1 big (26 to 28 inches long) loaf French bread

6 tablespoons Creole or whole grain mustard

6 tablespoons Mayonnaise

1/2 pound provolone cheese, thinly sliced

Directions

1. In a large mixing bowl, combine the ground meats, chopped yellow onion, chopped garlic, green onions, egg, bread crumbs, Worcestershire, 1 teaspoon of the salt and 1/2 teaspoon of the cayenne. Mix properly with your hands and form into 16 meatballs. Insert a garlic clove in the center of each meatball and pinch the meat around it.

2. Combine the flour and Creole seasoning (or cayenne pepper) in a shallow plate. Roll the meatballs equally in the flour mixture, tapping off any excess. Reserve any remaining flour.

3. In a big skillet, heat the oil over medium heat. Add the brown and meatballs evenly, using a spoon to turn them. Set aside the meatballs after removing it from the pan. With a wooden spoon, clean the bottom of the pan to loosen any brown bits. Stir in the reserved seasoned flour. Stir constantly for about 3 to 4 minutes to make a dark brown roux. Add the sliced onions and season with the left 1/2 teaspoon salt and 1/4 teaspoon cayenne. Cook and stirring constantly, until the onions are slightly soft, about 2 minutes. Gently pour in the beer and water and mix well. Return the meatballs to the skillet after you bring to boil. Reduce the heat to medium-low and simmer, uncovered, for about 1 hour, until the gravy is thick, turning and basting the meatballs with the pan gravy about every 15 minutes.

4. Remove from the heat and skim off any fat that has risen to the surface.

5. Cut the loaf of bread lengthwise in half. Place one half with the mustard and the other half with the mayonnaise. Place properly the provolone on the bottom half of the bread, overlapping the slices, then place the meatballs on top of the cheese. Spoon the gravy over the meatballs Top with the remaining bred half, cut into 6 equal portions, and serve immediately.

Why Sandwiches Are Beneficial For You

Due to their overall simplicity and that fact that there are literally hundreds of combinations out there, sandwiches tend to be the go-to meal for most people. Sandwiches themselves can become one a unique creation that you can throw together in minutes, there are many advantages to making them for yourself. In this section you will learn about the advantages of sandwiches and how it can help benefit you in the long run.

(1)Easy to Make

With the use of sandwiches, you can make yourself a filling and satisfying meal in just a matter of minutes. There is also no special skill that is required to make sandwiches. Not only is it great for those who can't really cook for themselves, but it is great for those who are tight on time when it comes to cooking and prepping your food.

(2)Can Easily Feed a Large Group of People

With the use of sandwiches, you can also feed a large group of people while saving money at the same time. Best of all you can make your own sandwiches to fit the needs and taste buds of those who are enjoying them.

(3)You Don't Need Any Utensils

One of the best things about sandwiches is the fact that you don't need any utensils in order to eat them. This will help to manage your time a bit better and give your piece of mind that you don't need to wash a sink full of dishes after making your sandwich.

(4)You Only Need A few Basic Ingredients

When you make sandwiches, you don't need any expensive or complicated ingredients. All you need is one to two toppings, some fresh bread or biscuits to make a sandwich. Feel free to use whatever ingredients fit into your budget.

(5)Sandwiches Are Portable

Another benefit to making sandwiches for yourself is the fact that they are portable. This means that regardless of whether or not you have a chaotic schedule, you can grab a bite and keep on going any time of the day.

Delicious Sandwich Recipes

Recipe 1: Loaded Turkish Style Grilled Cheese

This is a delicious sandwich recipe to make if you are looking for a unique and exotic sandwich dish to enjoy. Once you get a taste of this sandwich yourself, you will swear this is the best grilled cheese sandwich you can ever enjoy.

Yield: 1 Serving

Preparation Time: 20 Minutes

List of Ingredients:

- 1, 5 Ounce Roll of Bread, Kumru Variety
- 1 Tablespoon of Butter, Soft
- 3 Ounces of Sausage, Sucuk Variety, Casing Removed and Thinly Sliced
- 2 ¼ Ounce of Cheese, Kasseri Variety and Sliced Thinly
- 3 Pickle Spears, Small and Size and Sour Variety
- ¼ Cup of Hot Peppers, Pickled Variety and Sliced Thickly
- 4 Slices of Tomato, Roma Variety and Thinly Sliced

Instructions:

1. First slice your bread in half and spread the insides of your bread with your soft butter.

2. Then heat up a large sized skillet over medium to high heat. Once your skillet is hot enough grill your bread with the butter side facing down until lightly toasted. This should take at least 5 minutes. Remove from your skillet and set aside for later use.

3. Next cook up your sausages in your skillet. Cook for at least three minutes on each side or until crispy and brown in color. Once cooked remove your sausages from your skillet and place onto the bottom half of your roll.

4. Next lay your cheese directly onto your skillet and allow it to melt slightly in your sausage fat. Grill for at least 4 minutes before flipping. Continue grilling for another 3 minutes on the other side before removing and placing over your sausage.

5. Top off your sandwich with your tomato, pickles and peppers. Serve right away and enjoy.

Recipe 2: Healthy Stir-Fried Veggie Sandwich

This is a mayonnaise based veggie sandwich that is one of the healthiest sandwich dishes that you can enjoy today. Pack full of flavor and packed full of delicious taste, this is one sandwich recipe your family are going to be begging for.

Yield: 2 Servings

Preparation Time: 20 Minutes

List of Ingredients:

- ¼ Cup of Mayonnaise, Your Favorite Kind
- ¼ Cup of Rocoto Paste
- 1 teaspoon of Lime Juice, Fresh
- 2 tablespoons of Olive Oil, Extra Virgin Variety
- 1 Red Onion, Medium in Size and Thinly Sliced
- 1 Green Pepper, Medium in Size, Stemmed, Seeded and Sliced Thinly

- 1 Pepper, Banana or Amarillo Variety, Stemmed, Seeded and Sliced Thinly
- 6 Mushrooms, White Button Variety, Stemmed and Sliced Thinly
- 2 Cloves of Garlic, Chopped Finely
- 1 Piece of Ginger, Peeled and Chopped Finely
- 1 Tablespoon of Soy Sauce, Your Favorite Kind
- 1 Tablespoon of Vinegar, White Wine Variety
- 1 Tomato, Ripe, Cored, Seeded and Sliced Thinly
- Dash of Salt and Black Pepper, For Taste
- 4 Slices of Cheese, Monterey Jack Variety
- 2 Ciabatta Buns, Split Open and Lightly Toasted
- 1 Cup of Arugula, Fresh
- ¼ Cup of Cilantro, Fresh and Roughly Chopped

Instructions:
1. First add your favorite kind of mayonnaise, rocoto and fresh lime juice into a small sized bowl. Stir to thoroughly combine and set aside for later use.
2. Next heat up some oil in a large sized skillet placed over high heat. Once your oil is hot enough add in your onions and sliced peppers into it. Cook for the next 8 minutes or until soft to the touch. Transfer this mixture into a large sized bowl after this time.
3. Next add your mushrooms and cook for the next 2 to 3 minutes or until lightly brown in color.

4. Add in your garlic and ginger and continue to cook for another minute or two. After this time add in your favorite kind of soy sauce and vinegar. Cook for at least 30 seconds. Transfer this mixture to your bowl of onions and peppers and stir to combine.

5. Add your tomatoes to this bowl and season with a dash of salt and black pepper. Toss again to combine.

6. Place at least two slices of your cheese onto the bottom portions of your buns. Top off with half of your veggie mixture.

7. Pour your rocoto sauce over your veggies and top off with your fresh cilantro and arugula. Top off with your top portions of your buns and enjoy right away.

Recipe 3: Roasted Sweet Potato Sandwich With Rajas Salsa

This delicious sandwich recipe is packed full of sweet potatoes and makes for a delicious vegetarian sandwich to enjoy whenever you wish. Has a bit of a spicy taste that I know you won't be able to get enough of.

Yield: 2 Servings

Preparation Time: 40 Minutes

List of Ingredients:

- 1 Pound of Sweet Potatoes, Peeled and Thinly Sliced
- 1 Tablespoon of Olive Oil, Extra Virgin Variety
- 1 teaspoon of Cumin, Ground
- ½ teaspoon of Ancho Chile, Powdered Variety
- Dash of Salt and Pepper, For Taste
- 2 ½ teaspoon of Lime Juice, Fresh
- 2 tablespoons of Cilantro, Fresh and Minced
- 15 Tomatoes, Cherry Variety and Cut into Quarters

- 6 Peppers, Cherry Variety and Sliced Thinly
- 2 Peppers, Poblano Variety, Roasted and Thinly Sliced
- ¼ Cup of Sour Cream
- 2 Hoagie Rolls, Your Favorite Kind

Instructions:

1. Preheat your oven to 400 degrees.
2. While your oven is heating up toss your potatoes with your oil, cumin, powdered chile, dash of salt and pepper in a large sized bowl and transfer to a large sized baking dish.
3. Place in your oven to bake for the next 20 minutes or until fully brown in color.
4. Next use a small sized bowl and add in at least 2 tablespoons of your fresh lime juice, fresh cilantro, tomatoes, diced peppers and dash of salt and pepper. Stir thoroughly to combine.
5. Use a separate small sized bowl and add in your remaining lime juice and your sour cream. Stir to combine.
6. Then assemble your sandwich. To do this layer the bottom halves of your hoagie rolls with your sweet potatoes, fresh made salsa, fresh cilantro leaves and fresh sour cream. Top off with your top halves of your hoagie rolls. Serve whenever you are ready and enjoy.

Recipe 4: Classic Monte Cristo

Here is a classic sandwich recipe I know you are going to love to make. It is a double decker sandwich dish that you can make when you are looking for something more on the filling side.

Yield: 2 Servings

Preparation Time: 15 Minutes

List of Ingredients:
- ¼ Cup of Milk, Whole
- 2 Eggs, Large in Size
- Dash of Salt and Black Pepper, For Taste
- 5 tablespoons of Butter, Unsalted and Soft
- 6 Pieces of Bread, White Variety and Sliced Thinly
- 4 Slices of Turkey, Fully Cooked and Thinly Sliced
- 4 Slices of Ham, Fully Cooked and Thinly Sliced
- 4 Slices of Swiss Cheese, Thinly Sliced
- Dash of Sugar, Confectioner's Variety and for Garnish

- Some Red Jelly, Currant Variety and for Serving

Instructions:
1. The first thing that you will want to do is beat your milk and eggs together lightly in a small sized bowl. Season this mixture with a dash of salt and black pepper. Set aside for later use.
2. Next butter slices of bread on both sides with some soft butter. Place 2 slices of your turkey and ham between two slices of bread. Top off with two slices of cheese and then top off with some buttered bread. Trim the crusts and secure with a toothpick. Cut your sandwich in half.
3. Then melt your butter in a large sized skillet placed over medium heat. Dip your sandwich in your milk mixture until thoroughly coated. Place your coated sandwiches onto your skillet and fry until golden brown in color on both sides. This should take at least two minutes on each side.
4. Transfer your sandwich to a place and sprinkle with some confectioner's sugar. Serve with your red jelly and enjoy right away.

Recipe 5: Filling Pork Belly Gyro

While pork belly may seem far from appetizing, you won't think the same once you get a taste of this recipe for yourself. For the tastiest results make sure your pork belly is cut to the exact thickness that you desire.

Yield: 2 Servings

Preparation Time: 1 Hour and 30 Minutes

List of Ingredients:
- 1 Pound of Pork Belly, Boneless and Skinless Variety
- 1 Tablespoon of Garlic, Powdered Variety
- ½ Tablespoon of Marjoram, Dried Variety
- ½ Tablespoon of Rosemary, Dried Variety
- ½ Tablespoon of Thyme, Dried Variety
- ½ Tablespoon of Black Pepper, For Taste
- ½ Tablespoon of Cumin, Ground Variety
- ¼ teaspoon of Za'atar
- 1 Shallot, Thinly Sliced
- ¼ Cup of Yogurt, Fat Free and Greek Variety

- ¼ Cup of Sour Cream
- 1 teaspoon + 1 Tablespoon of Lemon Juice, Fresh
- ½ teaspoon of Oregano, Minced
- 1 Cucumber, Sliced Thinly
- 1 teaspoon of Salt, For Taste
- 2 tablespoons of Sugar, White in Color
- 1 teaspoon of Sumac
- ½ Cup of Romaine Lettuce, Freshly Shredded
- 1 Tomato, Plum Variety, Cored and Roughly Chopped
- 1 Lemon Rind, Minced
- 2 Pita Pockets, Cut into Halves

Instructions:

1. First preheat your oven to 275 degrees.
2. While your oven is heating up place your pork belly onto a large sized baking dish lined with some aluminum foil.
3. Then mix together your dash of black pepper, powdered garlic, fresh rosemary, fresh thyme, marjoram, ground cumin and za'atar into a small sized bowl. Stir thoroughly to combine. Rub this mixture onto your pork belly.
4. Place your pork into your oven to roast for the next 40 minutes. After this time increase the heat of your oven to 375 degrees and continue to roast for an additional 40 minutes. After this time remove and

allow to cool completely. Once cooled slice your pork belly into thin strips.

5. Next heat up a large sized skillet over high heat. Add in your shallots once your skillet is hot enough and cook for at least 10 to 12 minutes or until fully charred. Remove and allow to cool before adding into a medium sized bowl.

6. Then add in your yogurt, sour cream, fresh lemon juice, fresh oregano, fresh cucumber and dash of salt and pepper into your bowl. Stir thoroughly until evenly mixed and set aside for later use.

7. Use another medium sized bowl and add in your thinly sliced cucumber, white sugar, dash of salt and sumac into it. Stir to combine and allow to sit for the next 10 minutes. Add in your remaining ingredients and toss to combine.

8. Assemble your sandwiches. To do this stuff your pita halves with your cooked pork belly, fresh made tzatziki, sliced cucumber and lettuce mixture. Serve right away and enjoy.

Recipe 6: Italian Style Pulled Pork Sandwich

This is a classic and popular sandwich that is typically served in Philadelphia and now you can make it within the comfort of your own household. Packed full of herb braised pork, sharp provolone cheese and hot peppers to make a filling sandwich that you won't be able to get enough of.

Yield: 8 Servings

Preparation Time: 3 Hours and 15 Minutes

List of Ingredients:
- 3 tablespoons of Fennel Seeds, Ground Variety
- 3 tablespoons of Parsley, Fresh and Dried
- 1 ½ Tablespoon of Thyme, Fresh and Dried
- 3 ½ teaspoon of Red Chile Flakes, Crushed
- 1, 6 to 7 Pound Pork Shoulder, Cut Butterfly Style
- 3 Sprigs of Rosemary, Stemmed and Chopped Finely
- 1 Head of Garlic, Chopped Finely
- Dash of Salt and Black Pepper, For Taste

- 4 Cups of Beef Stock, Homemade Preferable
- ½ Cup of Red Wine, Your Favorite Kind
- 1 Onion, Yellow in Color and Sliced Thinly
- 1 Bay Leaf, Fresh
- ½ Cup of Tomatoes, Canned Variety and Crushed
- 2 Pounds of Broccoli Rabe, Fresh
- ¼ Cup of Oil, Canola Variety
- 32 Slices of Provolone Cheese, Thinly Sliced
- 8 Sandwich Rolls, Italian Variety and Split Open
- 24 Hot Peppers, Roasted Variety

Instructions:

1. Preheat your oven to 450 degrees.

2. While your oven is heating up add your fennel, fresh parsley, fresh thyme and crushed chili flakes into a small sized bowl. Stir thoroughly to combine and set aside for later use.

3. Then place your pork shoulder onto a flat surface and spread half of your herb mixture onto it. Also add your rosemary at least one quarter of your garlic and dash of salt and pepper. Roll up your pork should and tie with some kitchen twine. Season the outside of your pork should with your remaining herb mixture and dash of salt and pepper.

4. Place your pork onto a large sized roasting pan. Place into your oven to bake for the next 40 minutes or until brown in color. After this time remove your pork from your oven and set your oven to broil.

5. Add your remaining garlic to your pan along with your homemade stock, wine, onions and fresh bay leaf. Place your fresh tomatoes over your pork.

6. Place into your oven to broil for the next 20 minutes or until your tomatoes are caramelized. Then reduce the heat of your oven to 325 degrees. Cover your pork with some parchment paper and cover with some aluminum foil. Place back into your oven to bake for the next 2 hours. Remove and set aside completely to cool.

7. Transfer your pork to a cutting board and slice thinly. Meanwhile transfer your juice from your pork into a blender. Blend on the highest setting until smooth in consistency and transfer into a small sized saucepan. Set over low heat and keep warm. Add your pork to your warm pan juices.

8. Next bring a large sized pot of water to a boil. Once boiling add in your fresh broccoli. Cook for the next 2 to 3 minutes or until tender to the touch. After this time drain and set aside to cool completely. Pat dry with a few paper towels.

9. Heat up some oil in a large sized skillet set over medium heat. Add in your broccoli rabe and crushed red pepper flakes. Cook for the next 4 minutes or until crispy. Set aside for later use.

10. Place your provolone cheese onto the bottom halves of your roll. Top off with your cooked pork along with your crispy broccoli rave and peppers. Top off with the top half of your roll and serve right away.

Recipe 7: Tuna And Lemon Caper Sandwich

This brine filled and tangy sandwich is one that any seafood lover is going to enjoy. For the tastiest results I highly recommend letting this sandwich sit for a couple of minutes after you put it together.

Yield: 2 Servings

Preparation Time: 30 Minutes

Ingredients for Your Pickled Fennel:

- ¼ Cup of Vinegar, Rice Wine Variety
- 3 tablespoons of Sugar, White in Color
- 1 teaspoon of Salt, For Taste
- 1 Bulb of Fennel, Trimmed and Cut into Small Sized Pieces

Ingredients for Your Sandwich:

- ¼ Cup of Capers, Drained and Minced
- 6 Tablespoon of Olive Oil, Extra Virgin Variety

- 2 tablespoons of Chives, Minced
- 1 ½ Tablespoon of Mustard, Dijon Variety
- 2, 4 Ounce Cans of Tuna, In Water and Drained
- 2 Lemons, Fresh, Zest and Juice Only
- 2 Sprigs of Rosemary, Minced
- Dash of Salt and Black Pepper, For Taste
- ½ of a Baguette, Whole Wheat Variety and Cut into Half
- Some Arugula, Baby Variety and for Serving

Instructions:

1. The first thing that you will want to do is make your pickled fennel. To do this use a medium sized saucepan and add in your vinegar, white sugar, dash of salt and at least half a cup of water. Stir thoroughly and cook for the next 3 minutes or until your sugar has fully dissolves.

2. Pour this mixture over your fennel and allow to cool completely.

3. Next make your sandwich. To do this add at least 1/3 cup of your pickled fennel, capers, olive oil, fresh chives, Dijon mustard, fresh lemon juice and zest, drained tuna, fresh rosemary and dash of salt and pepper into a medium sized bowl. Stir thoroughly to combine.

4. Spread your tuna salad onto one side of your halved baguette and top off with your fresh arugula and

freshly made tapenade. Top off with the top half of your baguette and serve right away.

Recipe 8: Filling Spam And Cheese Sandwich

This is a great tasting sandwich to make whenever you are on a strict budget. Made with slider buns and smothered in Monterey and Cheddar cheese, this is one dish you won't regret making for yourself.

Yield: 8 Servings

Preparation Time: 15 Minutes

List of Ingredients:
- 1, 12 Ounce Can of SPAM
- ½ Cup of Mayonnaise, Your Favorite Kind
- 2 tablespoons of Milk, Coconut Variety
- 2 tablespoons of Sesame Seeds, Lightly Toasted
- 1 Tablespoon of Oil, Canola Variety
- 8 Potato Rolls, Split Open
- 1 Cup of Cheddar Cheese, Finely Shredded
- 1 Cup of Monterey Jack Cheese, Finely Shredded
- 8 tablespoons of Chili Sauce, Sweet Variety
- 4 teaspoons of Hot Sauce, Your Favorite Kind

- 8 tablespoons of Cabbage Kimchi, Roughly Chopped
- 8 teaspoons of Cilantro, Fresh and Roughly Chopped

Instructions:
1. The first thing that you will want to do is slice your spam into 8 equal sizes. Set aside for later use.
2. Then use a small sized bowl and add in your favorite kind of mayonnaise, milk and toasted sesame seeds. Stir thoroughly to combine and set aside for later use.
3. Heat up some oil in a large sized skillet placed over medium to high heat. Once your skillet is hot enough add in your SPAM and cook for the next 8 to 10 minutes or until thoroughly brown in color. Remove and set on a plate lined with paper towels to drain.
4. Next toast your rolls in your skillet until lightly brown. This should take at least one to two minutes at most.
5. Then preheat your oven to 350 degrees.
6. While your oven is heating up assemble your sandwiches. Spread your coconut mayonnaise mixture onto both sides of your bread. Top off with your cheese, at least two slices of cooked spam, at least one spoonful of your chili sauce, half a teaspoon of your hot sauce, at least one spoonful of your cabbages and at least one teaspoon of your fresh cilantro. Cover with the top buns.

7. Place your buns onto a large sized baking sheet and place into your oven to bake for the next 3 to 4 minutes or until the cheese is fully melted.
8. Remove from your oven and serve right away.

Recipe 9: Tasty Pimento Cheese Sandwich With Homemade Pickles

With the use of this recipe, you will want to enjoy the cheesy goodness on other treats instead of just the sandwich. For the tastiest results I highly recommend add some Sriracha to the cheese to make it a bit spicy.
Yield: 2 Servings

Preparation Time: 15 Minutes

List of Ingredients:

- 6 Ounces of Cheddar Cheese, Sharp Variety and Finely Shredded
- 6 Tablespoons of Aioli, Garlic Variety
- 2 teaspoons of Sriracha
- 1 teaspoon of Vinegar, Apple Cider Variety

- ¾ teaspoon of Paprika
- ¾ teaspoon of Worcestershire Sauce
- 2 Scallions, Minced
- 1 Red Bell Pepper, Peeled, Seeded, Minced and Roasted Variety
- Dash of Salt and Black Pepper, For Taste
- 4 Slices of Sandwich Bread, White in Color
- Some Homemade Pickles, For Serving
- Some Iceberg Lettuce, Finely Shredded and for Serving

Ingredients for Your Homemade Pickles:

- 1 ½ Pound of Cucumbers, Pickled Variety and Cut into Spears
- 6 Sprigs of Dill, Fresh
- 1 Onion, Yellow in Color and Sliced Thinly
- 3 Cups of Vinegar, White in Color
- 3 tablespoons of Sugar, White in Color
- 3 tablespoons of Coriander Seeds
- 1 Tablespoon of Fennel Seeds
- 1 Tablespoon of Mustard, Seeds Only

Instructions for Your Homemade Pickles:

1. Using two sterilized 1-quart jars, add in your fresh cucumber spears, fresh dill and onion.
2. Then use a small sized saucepan and add in your vinegar, white sugar, half a cup of your water,

coriander, fennel and mustard seeds into it. Stir thoroughly and bring your mixture to a boil.

3. Pour this mixture over your veggies in your jars and cover. Allow to sit for at least 24 hours before serving.

Instructions for Your Sandwich:

1. Using a large sized bowl add in your shredded cheese, aioli, vinegar, dash of paprika, Worcestershire sauce, Sriracha sauce, roasted peppers, scallions and dash of salt and pepper. Stir until thoroughly mixed together.

2. Spread your pimento cheese mixture over one slice of your bread. Top off with your homemade pickle, finely shredded lettuce and the top half of your bread. Serve whenever you are ready and enjoy.

Recipe 10: California Style Sandwich

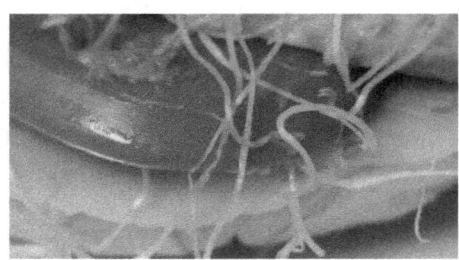

Just as the name implies this is a classic Californian dish to enjoy even if you are not from California. It is made using a combination of healthy vegetables on top of whole wheat bread to make not only a delicious sandwich, but a healthy one as one.

Yield: 2 Servings

Preparation Time: 12 Minutes

List of Ingredients:
- ¼ Cup of Buttermilk, Whole
- ¼ Cup of Sour Cream
- ¼ Cup of Mayonnaise, Your Favorite Kind
- 1 Tablespoon of Chives, Fresh and Finely Chopped
- 1 Tablespoon of Parsley, Fresh and Finely Chopped
- ½ teaspoon of Garlic, Powdered Variety
- ¼ teaspoon of Onion, Powdered Variety
- Dash of Salt and Black Pepper, For Taste
- 4 Slices of Sandwich Bread, Multigrain Variety
- 2 Slices of Cheese, Monterey Jack Variety

- ½ Cup of Alfalfa Sprouts, Fresh
- 1 Avocado, Fresh, Peeled, Pitted and Sliced Thinly
- 1 Tomato, Ripe, Cored and Thinly Sliced

Instructions:

1. The first thing that you are going to want to do is place your whole buttermilk, sour cream, favorite kind of mayonnaise, fresh chives, fresh parsley and powdered onion and garlic. Whisk thoroughly until evenly combined.
2. Season with a dash of salt and pepper. Spread this mixture onto all of your bread slices.
3. Place at least one slice of cheese onto your bread slices. Top off with your fresh alfalfa sprouts, fresh avocado and thinly sliced tomato. Season with a dash of salt and pepper.
4. Cover with your remaining bread slice and serve right away.

Recipe 11: Salvadoran Turkey Sandwich

If you are looking for something more on the exotic side, then this is the perfect sandwich recipe for you to make. This is a gently spiced turkey sandwich that I know you won't be able to resist.

Yield: 6 Servings

Preparation Time: 2 Hours and 50 Minutes

List of Ingredients:
- 1 ½ Cups of Beer, Light Variety
- 2 tablespoons of Olive Oil, Extra Virgin Variety
- 2 teaspoons of Peppercorns, Black in Color
- 2 teaspoons of Sesame Seeds
- 2 teaspoons of Pepitas
- 1 teaspoon of Oregano, Dried
- ½ teaspoon of Annatto Seeds
- 5 Cloves of Garlic, Minced
- 2 Bay Leaves, Fresh and Dried
- 2 Turkey Drumsticks, Large in Size

- Dash of Salt and Pepper, For Taste
- 2 Onions, Yellow in Color, 1 Finely Chopped and 1 Sliced Thinly
- 4 Tomatoes, Cored and Finely Chopped
- 1 Bell Pepper, Green in Color, Cored, Seeded and Finely Chopped
- 6 Bread Loaves, Italian Variety, Ends Trimmed and Split in Half
- 1 Handful of Watercress

Instructions:

1. The first thing that you will want to do is preheat your oven to 350 degrees.
2. While your oven is heating up add your water, light beer, olive oil, black peppercorns, Pepitas, fresh oregano, dried bay leaves, minced garlic and annatto into a blend. Blend thoroughly until thoroughly pureed.
3. Then add to a large sized Dutch oven along with your turkey. Season with a dash of salt and pepper and set over medium heat. Bring this mixture to a boil and cover. Braise for at least 2 hours or until your turkey is tender to the touch.
4. Next add your tomatoes, onions, one cup of water and peppers into a blender. Blend on the highest setting until smooth in consistency.
5. Transfer your cooked turkey to a pan and allow to cool.

6. Add your pureed tomato mixture into your Dutch oven and set over medium to high heat. Cook for the next 45 minutes or until thick in consistency.

7. Remove the meat of your turkey from the bones and cut into small sized pieces. Add your turkey into your sauce and reduce the heat to low. Cook for the next 5 minutes.

8. Season with a dash of salt and pepper. Remove from heat.

9. Serve with a garnish of onions and your watercress. Enjoy.

Recipe 12: Brazilian Style Roast Beef Sandwich

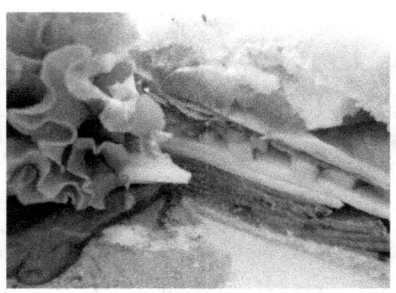

If you are a huge fan of roast beef, then this is going to become one of your favorite kind of sandwiches. Packed full of melted mozzarella cheese and topped off with fresh tomatoes, this is one dish you will want to make as often as possible.

Yield: 1 Serving

Preparation Time: 10 Minutes

List of Ingredients:

- 1, 6 Inch Roll, Portuguese Variety and Crusty
- 4 Slices of Roast Beef, Deli Variety
- 3 Slices of Tomato, Fresh and Ripe
- 6 Pickles Chips, Dill Variety
- 2 Slices of Mozzarella Cheese, Fresh

Instructions:

1. The first thing that you will want to do is preheat your oven to 350 degrees.

2. While your oven is heating up split your roll lengthwise and top off the bottom half of your roast beef, fresh tomato slices, dill pickle chips and fresh slices of mozzarella.

3. Cover with the top bun and place onto a large sized baking sheet. Place into your oven to bake until your cheese is fully melted. This should take at least 5 minutes.

4. Remove from your oven and allow to sit for at least one minute before serving while piping hot.

Recipe 13: Fried Mozzarella Sandwiches

These tiny fried sandwiches are great to enjoy if you are looking for something more on the savory side. Dripping with molten cheese, this is one sandwich you will want to enjoy over and over again.

Yield: 4 Servings

Preparation Time: 15 Minutes

List of Ingredients:
- Some Oil, Canola Variety and for Frying
- 6 Ounces of Mozzarella, Thinly Sliced
- 8 Slices of Sandwich Bread, White in Color
- Dash of Salt and Black Pepper, For Taste
- ½ Cup of Flour, All Purpose Variety
- 2 Eggs, Large in Size and Beaten Lightly
- 1 Cup of Breadcrumbs, Plain Variety

Instructions:

1. The first thing that you will want to do is pour your oil into a medium sized Dutch oven. Place over medium to high heat and heat up until it reaches 350 degrees.

2. Next divide your mozzarella cheese among 4 slices of bread. Season with a dash of salt and pepper. Cover with your remaining bread slices.

3. Trim the crusts of your sandwich and cut them into halves.

4. Place your flour into one small sized bowl, your beaten eggs in another small sized bowl and your breadcrumbs into another small sized bowl.

5. Then dredge your sandwiches in your flour, followed by dipping them into your eggs and last coating them in your breadcrumbs.

6. Place into your hot oil and fry for at least 2 minutes or until golden brown in color.

7. Remove and drain on a plate lined with paper towels and serve whenever you are ready.

Recipe 14: Simple Honey And Ricotta Sandwich

Here is yet another simple and absolutely delicious sandwich recipe that I know you will want to make whenever you are feeling particularly lazy. Made with sweet honey this is a great tasting sandwich recipe to make if you need to satisfy your strongest sweet tooth.

Yield: 1 Serving

Preparation Time: 5 Minutes

List of Ingredients:

- 2 Slices of Bread, Oat or Oatmeal Variety
- 3 tablespoons of Ricotta Cheese, Soft
- 1 teaspoon of Honey, Sourwood Variety
- ¼ teaspoon of Red Pepper Flakes, Crushed Variety

Instructions:

1. The first thing that you will want to do is toast your bread lightly on both sides in your toaster until golden in color.

2. Then spread some ricotta cheese on one side of your bread. Top off with a drizzling of your honey and a dash of crushed red pepper flakes.

3. Top off with your remaining slice of bread and serve right away.

Recipe 15: Buttermilk Style Fried Chicken Sandwich

If you are a huge fan of classic fried chicken, then this is one sandwich I know you are going to love. This sandwich is made by dredging your chicken in some buttermilk to make the juiciest fried chicken you can ever enjoy.

Yield: 2 Servings
Preparation Time: 1 Hour and 20 Minutes

List of Ingredients:

- 1 Cup of Buttermilk, Whole
- Dash of Salt and Black Pepper, For Taste
- 2, 4 Ounce Chicken Breasts, Boneless and Skinless Variety
- 2 ¼ tsp + ½ Cup of Vinegar, Red Wine Variety
- 1 teaspoon of Mustard, Dijon Variety
- 2 tablespoons of Olive Oil, Extra Virgin Variety
- 1 Red Onion, Small in Size and Sliced Thinly
- 2 Cups of Green Cabbage, Fresh and Sliced Thinly

- 2 tablespoons of Parsley, Minced
- 2 Jalapenos, Stemmed, De-Seeded and Sliced Thinly
- 1 Cup of Flour, All Purpose Variety
- ½ teaspoon of Cayenne Pepper
- Some Oil, Canola Variety and for Frying
- 2 Ciabatta Rolls, Sliced in Half

Instructions:

1. Add your buttermilk and dash of salt and pepper into a medium sized bowl. Whisk until thoroughly combined. Add your chicken to this mixture and toss thoroughly to coat. Cover with some plastic wrap and place into your fridge to chill for at least one hour.

2. Ad your vinegar, mustard and dash of salt and pepper into a large sized bowl. Whisk thoroughly and while you are whisking, drizzle your olive oil in. Set this mixture aside for later use.

3. Add in at least half cup of your vinegar and onion into a medium sized bowl. Allow to sit for the next 5 minutes. After this time drain your onions.

4. Add your onions, cabbages, fresh parsley, sliced jalapenos and dash of salt and pepper to your reserved vinaigrette, making sure to toss thoroughly to combine. Cover your mixture with some plastic wrap and place into your fridge to chill until you begin to assemble your sandwiches.

5. Use a shallow bowl and add in your flour, cayenne pepper and dash of salt and pepper. Stir until evenly mixed.

6. Heat up your oil in a large sized frying pan and set over medium to high heat until your oil reaches 325 degrees. Once your oil is hot enough add your chicken into your flour, making sure to coat on all sides. Then dip your coated chicken into your buttermilk and roll again in your flour.

7. Add your chicken into your hot oil. Cook for the next 8 minutes or until golden brown in color on all sides. Remove and place onto a plate lined with paper towels to drain.

8. Season with a dash of salt and assemble your sandwiches next. To do this place your cooked chicken onto the bottom of your sandwich rolls. Top off with your homemade coleslaw and top off with the top halves of your sandwich rolls. Serve right away and enjoy.

Recipe 16: Simple Tomato Sandwich

If you are looking for a healthy and delicious simple sandwich recipe to put together, then this is the perfect sandwich for you to make. It is a great sandwich dish to make during the hot summer months and can be made in just a matter of minutes.

Yield: 1 Serving

Preparation Time: 5 Minutes

List of Ingredients:

- 1 Tomato, Ripe and Fresh
- Some Butter, Soft and for Spreading
- 2 Slices of Toast, Your Favorite Kind and Thinly Sliced
- Dash of Salt and Black Pepper, For Taste
- Some Sugar, White in Color

Instructions:

1. The first thing that you will want to do is slice your tomato. Then butter some of your toast and add a thick

layer of your favorite kind of mayonnaise on both of your pieces of bread.

2. Lay two to three slices of your tomato on your bread slices. Season with a generous amount of salt and pepper. Add a small pinch of white sugar.

3. Serve right away and enjoy.

Recipe 17: Chicken Schnitzel Sandwich Smothered In Horseradish Cream And Radicchio

This delicious sandwich is a creative twist on a classic fried chicken dish. The homemade horseradish cream helps to offset the bitter taste of the radicchio and helps to give this dish a rich and savory taste I know you will love.

Yield: 4 Servings

Preparation Time: 15 Minutes

List of Ingredients:

- 1 Cup of Sour Cream
- 3 tablespoons of Horseradish, Freshly Grated
- 2 teaspoons of Vinegar, Cider Variety
- 1 Head of Radicchio, Cored, Leaves Separated and Cut into Halves
- Dash of Salt and Black Pepper, For Taste
- 2 Cups of Oil, Canola Variety
- 2 Cups of Flour, All Purpose Variety

- 2 tablespoons of Paprika, Spanish Variety
- 1 teaspoon of Garlic, Powdered Variety
- 4 Eggs, Large in Size and Beaten Lightly
- 2 Cups of Breadcrumbs, Panko Variety
- 4 Chicken Thighs, Boneless and Skinless Variety
- 8 tablespoons of Butter, Unsalted Variety
- 1 Bunch of Rosemary, Fresh
- 1 Bunch of Thyme, Fresh
- 1 Loaf of Challah Bread, Toasted and Sliced Thinly
- Some Applesauce, Your Favorite Kind and for Serving

Instructions:
1. The first thing that you will want to do is make your horseradish cream. To do this add your sour cream, horseradish and vinegar in a small sized bowl. Whisk until evenly mixed.
2. Then use another small sized bowl and add in your remaining vinegar, radicchio and dash of salt and pepper. Stir again to combine and set aside for later use.
3. Heat up some oil in a large sized skillet placed over medium to high heat.
4. While your oil is heating up add your flour, paprika, powdered garlic and dash of salt and pepper into a medium sized bowl. Place your beaten eggs in another bowl and your panko breadcrumbs into another small sized bowl.

5. Dredge your chicken in your flour mixture, followed by dipping your chicken into your beaten eggs and coating last in your breadcrumbs.

6. Place your coated chicken into your hot oil and fry for at least 1 to 2 minutes or until your chicken is golden brown in color.

7. Place your soft butter, fresh rosemary and fresh thyme into a separate large sized skillet. Once your chicken has been fried transfer to this skillet and cook for the next 3 minutes or until crispy to the touch. Transfer your chicken onto a plate lined with paper towels and season with a dash of salt.

8. Spread a thin layer of your applesauce onto a slice of bread. Top off with a cooked piece of chicken followed by a topping of your radicchio. Spread your homemade horseradish cream over another slice of bread and place on top. Slice your sandwich in half and serve whenever you are ready. Enjoy.

Recipe 18: Hearty Porchetta Sandwiches

This is a great sandwich recipe to make whenever you are looking to impress and satisfy your significant other. It is a sandwich that is packed full of delicious pork and served on fresh ciabatta bread to make a sandwich that every person in your household will fall in love with.

Yield: 8 Servings

Preparation Time: 2 Hours and 30 Minutes

Ingredients for Your Porchetta:
- ½ Cup of Rosemary Leaves, Fresh and Packed Lightly
- ½ Cup of Sage Leaves and Packed Lightly
- 1/3 Cup of Olive Oil, Extra Virgin Variety
- 3 tablespoons of Fennel Seeds, Crushed Lightly
- 2 ½ Tablespoon of Black Pepper, For Taste
- 1 Tablespoon of Red Chile Flakes, Crushed
- 14 Cloves of Garlic, Sliced Thinly
- 1, 6 to 7 Pound Pork Shoulder, Skin on and Cut Butterfly Variety

- Dash of Salt, For Taste

Ingredients for Your Gremolata, Aioli Sauce and Serving:
- 1 1/3 Cups of Olive Oil, Extra Virgin Variety
- 1 Cup of Parsley Leaves, Fresh and Lightly Packed
- ½ Cup of Hazelnuts, Lightly Toasted
- 5 tablespoons of Capers, Packed, Drained and Rinsed
- 1 Tablespoon of Oil, Hazelnut Variety
- 1 Shallot, Small in Size and Thinly Sliced
- 2 Lemons, Fresh, Juice and Zest Only
- Dash of Salt and Black Pepper, For Taste
- 2 Eggs, Yolks Only and Large in Size
- 8 Ciabatta Buns, Split Open

Instructions:

1. The first thing that you will want to do is make your pork. To do this preheat your oven to 325 degrees. While your oven is heating up add your fresh rosemary, fresh sage, at least ¼ cup of your oil, fennel seeds, dash of black pepper, crushed chili flakes and garlic into a food processor. Blend on the highest setting until a paste begins to form.

2. Place your pork onto a cutting board and place the skin side down. Season with a dash of salt and spread your herb paste evenly over the surface. Roll it up and

tie off with some kitchen twine. Rub your pork with some oil.

3. Place your rolled up pork into a large sized baking dish and cover with some aluminum foil. Place into your oven to bake for the next hour and 45 minutes. After this remove the aluminum foil and increase the heat to broil. Broil your pork for the next 15 minutes or until the skin is brown in color and crispy.

4. After this time remove your pork from your oven and allow to rest for the next 15 minutes.

5. While your pork is cooking make your gremolata. To do this add at least 1/3 cup of oil, fresh parsley, fresh hazelnuts, at least 1 tablespoon of your capers, hazelnut style oil, shallots and juice and zest from one lemon into a food processor. Blend on the highest setting until smooth in consistency. Transfer to a medium sized bowl and set aside for later use.

6. Next make your aioli. To do this add your remaining capers, 2 tablespoons of your fresh lemon juice, large egg yolks and one spoonful of water into a medium sized bowl. Whisk until smooth in consistency.

7. While you are whisking your mixture make sure that you drizzle your remaining oil until your sauce is thick in consistency. Season this mixture with a dash of salt and pepper. Place into your fridge to chill until you are ready to use it.

8. Make your sandwich. To do this spread your freshly made aioli sauce on the tops of your ciabatta bread while spreading your gremolata on the bottoms of your

buns. Add your sliced pork shoulder among your buns and bring them together. Serve right away and enjoy.

Recipe 19: Bel Air Style Club Sandwich

This delicious sandwich dish is topped off with a fried egg and smothered in gooey Gruyere cheese, making it one sandwich dish I know you are going to want to enjoy over and over again. This is the perfect sandwich to make if you are looking for something on the classy side.

Yield: 1 Serving

Preparation Time: 12 Minutes

- List of Ingredients:
- ¼ Cup of Mayonnaise, Your Favorite Kind
- 2 teaspoons of Chervil, Minced
- 2 teaspoons of Chives, Minced
- 2 teaspoons of Parsley, Minced
- 2 teaspoons of Tarragon, Minced
- ½ of a Shallot, Small in Size and Minced
- Dash of Salt and Black Pepper, For Taste
- 1 Tablespoon of Oil, Canola Variety

- 1 Egg, Large in Size
- 3 Slices of Bread, White in Color, Crusts Removed and Toasted Lightly
- ½ an Ounce of Turkey, Maple Glazed Variety and Sliced Thinly
- ½ an Ounce of Ham, Smoked Variety and Sliced Thinly
- 2 Slices of Gruyere Cheese
- 3 Slices of Bacon, Thick Cut Variety and Fully Cooked
- ½ of a Tomato, Ripe, Cored and Sliced Thinly
- 2 Leaves of Lettuce, Romaine Variety
- Some French Fries, Fully Cooked and for Serving

Instructions:

1. Use a medium sized bowl and add in your favorite kind of mayonnaise, fresh chives, fresh parsley, chervil, minced tarragon, sliced shallot and dash of salt and pepper. Stir thoroughly to combine. Set your freshly aioli aside for later use.

2. Next heat up some oil in a large sized skillet placed over medium to high heat. Once your oil is hot enough fry up your egg, making sure to flip at least once. Cook until the white of your eggs is fully cooked through. This should take at least 1 to 2 minutes.

3. Once your egg is cooked remove from your skillet and season with a dash of salt and pepper. Set aside for later use.

4. Lay a slice of bread onto a flat surface. Spread at least one spoonful of your aioli onto the bread. Top off with your turkey, smoked ham and Gruyere cheese. Spread your remaining aioli sauce on the other side of bread and top off your sandwich, making sure the aioli side is facing up.

5. Top your aioli slice of bread with your fried egg, cooked bacon, tomato slices and a dash of salt and pepper. Top off with your lettuce leaves and another slice of aioli spread bread, with the aioli side facing down.

6. Serve your sandwich with some fries of your choice and enjoy right away.

Recipe 20: Soft Crab Sandwich Smothered With Collard Slaw

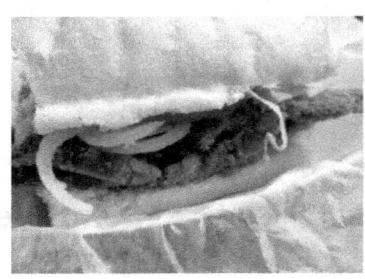

This is a perfect sandwich recipe to make if you are a huge fan of crab. It is packed full of a crispy and tangy tartar and cocktail sauce to make a sandwich recipe that you will want to make over and over again.

Yield: 4 Servings

Preparation Time: 5 Hours and 15 Minutes

Ingredients for Your Sauce and Slaw:

- ½ Cup of Mayonnaise, Your Favorite Kind
- 1 ½ teaspoon of Pickles, Bread and Butter Variety and Finely Chopped
- 1 ½ teaspoon of Lemon Juice, Fresh
- 1 ½ teaspoon of Onion, Sweet Variety and Minced
- ½ teaspoon of Garlic, Powdered Variety
- ½ teaspoon of Chile Flakes, Crushed
- ½ Cup of Ketchup, Your Favorite Kind
- 3 tablespoons of Horseradish, Fully Prepared

- 1 Tablespoon of Lemon Juice, Fresh
- 2 teaspoons of Hot Sauce, Asian Variety and Your Favorite Kind
- ½ Cup of Vinegar, Apple Cider Variety
- 3 tablespoons of Sugar, White in Color
- 2 tablespoons of Oil, Canola Variety
- ½ teaspoon of Celery Seed
- 1/8 teaspoon of Mustard, Dried Variety
- ½ Head of Green Cabbage, Small in Size and Finely Shredded
- 2 tablespoons of Parsley, Minced
- 6 Leaves of Collard Greens, Stemmed and Sliced Thinly
- 1 Carrots, Fresh, Peeled and Grated
- ½ of an Onion, Small in Size and Coarsely Grated
- Dash of Salt and Black Pepper, For Taste

Ingredients for Your Crabs:

- 8 Crabs, Softshell Variety and Cleaned
- Dash of Salt and Black Pepper, For Taste
- 2 Cups of Flour, All Purpose Variety
- 1/3 Cup of Olive Oil, Extra Virgin Variety
- 3 tablespoons of Butter, Soft and Unsalted Variety
- 4 Buns, Lightly Toasted

Instructions:

1. First make your tartar sauce. To do this use a small sized bowl and add in your favorite kind of mayonnaise, fresh lemon juice, pickles, sweet onions, powdered garlic, crushed chile flakes and dash of salt and pepper. Stir thoroughly until evenly mixed. Cover with some plastic wrap and place it into your fridge to chill for the next 3 hours.

2. Next make your cocktail sauce. To do this add your chili sauce, horseradish, fresh lemon juice and favorite hot sauce into a small sized bowl. Whisk until thoroughly combined. Cover with some plastic wrap and place into your fridge to chill for the next hour.

3. Then make your coleslaw. To do this use a medium sized bowl and add in your vinegar, white sugar, oil, fresh celery seeds and mustard. Stir thoroughly until evenly combined. Then add in your fresh parsley, fresh collard greens, fresh carrots, onions and dash of salt and black pepper. Stir again to combine. Cover with some plastic wrap and place into your fridge to chill for the next hour.

4. Cook your crabs after this time. To do this use a large sized bowl and add in your flour and dash of salt and pepper. Stir thoroughly to combine and set aside for later use. Coat your crabs completely in your flour mixture.

5. Heat up some oil and butter in a large sized skillet set over medium to high heat. Once your oil and butter is hot enough add in your crab and cook for the next 2

to 3 minutes or until golden brown in color. Remove and set onto a plate lined with paper towels to drain.

6. Assemble your sandwich. To do this slather your bread with your tartar and cocktail sauce on the inside of your buns. Top off with your fried crabs and homemade coleslaw. Serve right away and enjoy.

Recipe 21: Jersey Style Pork Roll Breakfast Sandwich

This is one of my personal favorite sandwich recipes and once you get a taste of it yourself, this will too become one of your favorite sandwiches. It is a highly popular sandwich in New Jersey, and I guarantee it will soon become a favorite breakfast sandwich in your household.

Yield: 1 Serving

Preparation Time: 10 Minutes

List of Ingredients:

- 1 Tablespoon of Butter, Soft and Unsalted Variety
- 4 Slices of Pork Roll, with Edges Scored

- 1 Egg, Large in Size
- 2 Slices of Cheese, American Variety
- 1 English Muffin, Lightly Toasted
- Some Ketchup, For Serving

Instructions:

1. First heat up some butter in a large sized skillet placed over medium heat. Once your butter is fully melted and your skillet is hot enough crack your egg into the skillet.

2. Add in your pork roll slices. Cook both your eggs and pork at the same time. Cook until your egg whites have set fully and your pork is lightly brown in color. This should take at least 3 minutes.

3. Top off your pork and egg with your slices of cheese. Allow to melt for the next minute.

4. Stack your pork rolls onto the bottom of your English muffin. Top off with your egg and your slices of cheese. Add your top portion of your English muffin and serve right away with some ketchup if you prefer. Enjoy.

Recipe 22: Filling Lemon, Ham And Cheese Sandwiches

While lemon may not seem like it would pair excellently with a ham and cheese sandwich, you will think differently once you get a taste of this sandwich for yourself. This sandwich has a pleasing tang flavor that you will love.

Yield: 4 Servings

Preparation Time: 2 Hours and 30 Minutes

Ingredients for Your Lemon Curd:
- ¾ Cup of Sugar, White in Color
- 4 Eggs, Yolks Only and Large in Size
- 12 tablespoons of Butter, Fully Melted and Unsalted Variety
- 3 Lemons, Zest and Juice Only

Ingredients for Your Sandwiches:
- 8 Slices of Brioche
- Some Butter, Melted and for Brushing

- 2 Ounces of Goat Cheese, Soft to The Touch
- 4 Eggs, Large in Size
- 1 teaspoon of Thyme, Fresh and Chopped Finely
- Dash of Salt and Black Pepper, For Taste
- 16 Slices of Ham, Black Forest Variety
- 4 Ounces of Mache

Instructions:

1. The first thing that you will want to do is make your curd. To do this add your white sugar and egg yolks into a small sized saucepan. Then add in your melted butter, fresh juice and zest and whisk thoroughly until smooth in consistency.

2. Place this saucepan over medium heat and cook for at least 8 to 10 minutes or until thick in consistency. After this time strain your curd into a small sized bowl. Wrap with some plastic wrap and place into your fridge to chill for the next 2 hours.

3. Next make your sandwich. To do this heat up a large sized skillet placed over medium to high heat. Bush one side of two slices of your brioche with some butter. Place into your hot skillet and toast for at least one minutes. Transfer these slices to a plate with the toasted side facing down.

4. Spread at least half an ounce of your goat cheese over your brioche. Top off with at least 2 ½ tablespoons of your lemon curd on the other slice.

5. Next whisk at least one egg in a small sized bowl. Add into your hot skillet and season with a dash of salt

and pepper and your fresh thyme. Cook until set before flipping. Cook for another 2 minutes before placing on top of your goat cheese on your brioche.

6. Place four slices of your ham next to your skillet and cook for at least 30 seconds to one minute. Flip and cook for the same time. Transfer on top of your omelet.

7. Top your omelet with at least one ounce of your mache and finally top with your lemon curd smothered bread slice. Repeat until all of your sandwiches have been made. Serve right away and enjoy.

Recipe 23: Classic Football Sandwiches

Just as the name implies these sandwiches are perfect to make during the football season. They are miniature in size and smothered in a tangy butter-poppy seed sauce that I know you are going to fall in love with.
Yield: 8 Servings
Preparation Time: 1 Hour and 5 Minutes

List of Ingredients:

- 8 Dinner Rolls, White in Color
- 12 Ounces of Cheese, Swiss Variety and Thinly Sliced
- 9 Ounces of Ham, Honey Variety and Sliced Thinly
- 1 Stick of Butter, Full Melted
- 2 tablespoons of Mustard, Fully Prepared and Dijon Variety
- 2 tablespoons of Poppy Seeds
- 1 teaspoon of Worcestershire Sauce

Instructions:

1. First slice your rolls in half and place the bottom rolls into a large sized casserole dish.
2. Place a layer of cheese on top of your rolls followed by a layer of your honey ham. Top off with your roll tops.
3. Next use a small sized bowl and add in your fully melted butter, Dijon mustard, poppy seeds and Worcestershire sauce. Whisk thoroughly until evenly combined. Drizzle this sauce over the top of your sandwiches.
4. Cover your dish with a sheet of aluminum foil. Allow to sit for the next 30 minutes.
5. After this time place your dish into your oven to bake at 350 degrees for the next 20 to 25 minutes or until your cheese is fully melted.
6. Remove and allow your sandwiches to sit for at least 5 minutes before serving.

Recipe 24: Cuban Style Medianoche Sandwich

This is the kind of sandwich you will want to enjoy after a hard night of partying. Made using hearty roasted pork, savory Swiss cheese and homemade pickles, this is one dish I know you will fall in love with.

Yield: 4 Servings

Preparation Time: 1 Hour

List of Ingredients:
- 1 Pound of Pork Loin
- Dash of Salt and Pepper, For Taste
- 2 tablespoons of Olive Oil, Extra Virgin Variety
- 4 Slices of Challah Bread, Fresh
- ½ Cup of Mustard, Yellow in Color
- 1 Pound of Ham, Deli Variety and Thinly Sliced
- 8 Slices of Swiss Cheese, Thinly Sliced
- 4 Pickles, Dill Variety
- 4 tablespoons of Butter, Soft and Unsalted Variety

Instructions:

1. The first thing that you will want to do is preheat your oven to 400 degrees. While your oven is heating up season your pork with a dash of salt and pepper. Drizzle some olive oil over the top and place into a roasting pan.
2. Place into your oven to bake for the next 45 minutes. After this time remove and transfer your pork loin onto a cutting board. Allow to rest for the next 15 minutes before slicing thinly.
3. Next slice your bread in half and spread the insides of your rolls with at least one spoonful of mustard. Top off with your ham, cooked pork, Swiss cheese and pickles.
4. Then heat up half of your butter in a large sized skillet placed over medium heat. Once your butter is fully melted add in your sandwiches and press slightly. Cook for the next 3 minutes or until the bottom of your sandwiches are golden in color.
5. Flip and continue to cook until the tops are golden brown in color. This should take at least 3 minutes.
6. Remove from your skillet and cut your sandwiches in half. Serve right away and enjoy.

Recipe 25: Tasty Smothered Pimento Cheese Braised Brisket Sandwiches

If you are looking for a particularly filling sandwich, then this is the perfect sandwich recipe for you to make. Hearty beef brisket smothered in melted pimento cheese makes one sandwich recipe you will want to make over and over again.

Yield: 8 to 10 Servings

Preparation Time: 6 Hours

List of Ingredients:

- 1 ½ teaspoon of Salt, For Taste
- 1 teaspoon of Black Pepper, For Taste
- ¼ teaspoon of Paprika
- 1, 3 ½ Pound of Beef Brisket
- 1 ½ Tablespoon of Oil, Vegetable Variety
- 1 Onion, Yellow in Color and Chopped Roughly

- 3 Cloves of Garlic, Minced
- 2 Tomatoes, Plum Variety, Cored and Chopped Roughly
- 2 Stalks of Celery, Fresh and Chopped Roughly
- 1 Carrot, Fresh and Chopped Roughly
- 1, 12 Ounce Bottle of Beer, Stout Variety
- 4 Cups of Beef Stock, Homemade Preferable
- ½ Cup of Bourbon
- ¼ Cup of Soy Sauce, Your Favorite Kind
- ¼ Cup of Brown Sugar, Light and Packed
- 1 Tablespoon of Vinegar, Balsamic Variety
- 1 Bunch of Thyme, Fresh and Chopped Roughly
- 8 Ounces of Cheddar Cheese, Freshly Grated
- 4 Ounces of Cheddar Cheese, while in Color and Freshly Grated
- ¾ Cup of Mayonnaise, Your Favorite Kind
- ¼ Cup of Gochujang
- 2 tablespoons of Parmesan Cheese, Freshly Grated
- ½ teaspoon of Worcestershire Sauce
- 1, 4 Ounce Jar of Peppers, Pimiento Variety and Chopped Finely
- 12 Slider Buns, Cut into Halves
- 6 Dill Pickles, Whole and Sliced Thinly

Instructions:
1. The first thing that you will want to do is preheat your oven to 325 degrees.

2. While your oven is heating use a small sized bowl and add in at least 1 ½ teaspoons of salt, 1 teaspoon of black pepper and your paprika. Stir to combine and rub this mixture over your beef brisket. Allow your brisket to stand for at least one hour.

3. Next heat up some oil in a large sized cast iron pot set over medium to high heat. Once your oil is hot enough add in your beef brisket and cook for the next 8 minutes or until thoroughly brown on all sides. After this time transfer your brisket to a plate.

4. Add your onions and two cloves of your garlic into your pot. Cook for the next 2 minutes before adding in your tomatoes, fresh celery and fresh carrots. Cook for the next 6 to 8 minutes or until soft to the touch.

5. Once soft add in your beer, homemade stock, bourbon, favorite kind of soy sauce, light brown sugar, vinegar and fresh thyme. Stir to combine and bring your mixture to a boil. Once your mixture is boiling reduce the heat to low and add your brisket into your pot.

6. Transfer your pot to your oven and cook in your oven for the next 3 ½ hours or until tender to the touch.

7. Add your remaining clove of garlic, both of your cheddar cheeses, favorite mayonnaise, gochujang, parmesan cheese and Worcestershire sauce into a food processor. Pulse on the highest setting until thoroughly combine. Transfer your mixture into a medium sized bowl and add in your pimientos. Stir to combine and

season with a dash of salt and pepper. Place into your fridge to chill until you are ready to serve it.

8. After this time remove your brisket from your oven and slice on a cutting board.

9. Pour your liquid back into your pot and bring to a boil over medium to high heat. Cook for the next 10 minutes or until reduced. This should take at least 20 minutes. Remove from heat and serve over your brisket. Enjoy.